P9-EDC-367

Integrating the Arts Across the Content Areas

Lisa Donovan, Ph.D.
Louise Pascale, Ph.D.

LESLEY UNIVERSITY

SHELL EDUCATION

Publishing Credits

Dona Herweck Rice, *Editor-in-Chief*; Robin Erickson, *Production Director*;
Lee Aucoin, *Creative Director*; Timothy J. Bradley, *Illustration Manager*;
Sara Johnson, *Senior Editor*; Tracy Edmunds, *Editor*; Leah Quillian, *Assistant Editor*;
Grace Alba, *Designer*; Corinne Burton, M.A.Ed., *Publisher*

Standards
© 2004 Mid-continent Research for Education and Learning (McREL)

Shell Education

5301 Oceanus Drive
Huntington Beach, CA 92649-1030
http://www.shelleducation.com
ISBN 978-1-4258-0845-7
©2012 Shell Educational Publishing, Inc.
Reprinted 2013

Table of Contents

Foreword

Engaging students, reaching diverse learners, closing achievement gaps, getting students to want to come to school—what educator doesn't face these challenges every day? Yet there are classrooms in districts across the country—urban, rural, suburban—where these challenges are fading as excitement in the classroom is taking hold. The common thread these classrooms share is that the curriculum is being taught through the arts, and that is making all the difference. Teachers who integrate the arts into their curriculum, whether they work in primary or secondary classrooms, tell the same story over and over: the student who would not pick up his pencil but will now not stop writing poetry; the students who were bored by animal adaptation but are now excited about science when drama became the teaching tool; and the class that can now learn and retain geometric concepts through creative movement. And what about the teachers themselves? Arts-integrated instruction reignited a spark they thought was gone.

How can teachers take the time to integrate the arts into their classrooms when it seems there is already not enough time to cover the curriculum? Every curricular change requires an investment in time, but a single modification can lead to a lifetime return of engaged, thoughtful, interested students. This is not an educational fad soon to be eclipsed by some new flavor-of-the-month educational strategy. The arts have proven themselves to be a tool through which academic performance improves across the curriculum. Now is the time to reignite creativity in the classroom for both teachers and students.

Integrating the Arts Across the Content Areas is an excellent guide to arts integration for teachers who wish to become more experienced in the arts. For the overwhelmed teacher who is having difficulty getting an ever-growing list of curriculum benchmarks nailed down, this book provides a roadmap to

Foreword *(cont.)*

"weaving [the arts] into the curriculum as a natural part of how the content is presented and assessed (Introduction, page 17)." For the teacher who was not born with a paintbrush in hand, there are activities for you to experience for yourself the cognitive awakening that the arts can provide for your students. For the teachers who find themselves uninspired after years of teaching the same curriculum, this book provides student activities that breathe fresh air into your instruction.

As good teachers do, Lisa Donovan and Louise Pascale invite you to dive in wherever your curiosity leads you. Integrating the Arts Across the Content Areas explores six art forms: poetry, music, storytelling, drama, visual art, and creative movement. Each chapter describes the art form, why it matters, makes connections to the Common Core State Standards and 21st century skills, and offers innovative, engaging student activities. Additionally, an entire chapter is dedicated to planning and assessment. The appendices provide a sample unit outline that integrated the arts, along with a planning chart template to get started. To extend learning, there is also an extensive list of resources for each art discipline.

Students need more opportunities to develop divergent thinking skills and to work with a variety of symbolic systems to access meaning and express understanding. Arts integration can act as a connective fabric between sequential learning in the content areas and extending opportunities for students to use their creative skills in a variety of capacities. Moreover, arts integration harnesses the innate ability of the arts to fully engage students. As you read this book, you will encounter a variety of teacher testimonials that share the incredible ability of the arts to excite and engage today's students.

—Diane Daily
Education Programs Manager
Massachusetts Cultural Council

Acknowledgments

This book was created with inspiration and input from many, many people, particularly Lesley University's Creative Arts in Learning Integrating Teaching through the Arts (ITA) Master's Degree students who generously shared their experiences integrating the arts with their students. Their input, enthusiasm, and wealth of experience have made this book much more meaningful and relevant. Thank you all.

Amanda Campbell, Rome, GA
Carol Schneider, Coeur d'Alene, ID
Christine Miller, Temecula, CA
Cindy Denny, Kenai, AL
Darlene Moody, St. George, UT
David McCormick, Raymond, NH
Elizabeth Thurgood, Coeur d'Alene, ID
Ellen Weissman, Coeur d'Alene, ID
Erica Lindholdt Duncan, Coeur d'Alene, ID
Jan Call, St. George, UT
Jason Morgan, Westbrook, ME
Jonathan Wheeler, Raymond, NH
Kalee Alexandria, Tacoma, WA
Kate DePalo, Raymond, NH
Katie Palmer, Coeur d'Alene, ID
Keri Cook, Cumming, GA
Kerry Erwin, Coeur d'Alene, ID
Kimberly Magyar, Green Bay, WI
Kirsten Eichenauer, Cambridge, MA
Kristy Landsem, Las Vegas, NV
Layne Stone, Rome, GA
Leah Jaeks, Green Bay, WI
Lori Lubkeski, Cambridge, MA
Melissa Webster, Westbrook, ME
Mike Rosenthal, Great Barrington, MA
Molly LaFavor, Seattle, WA
Nancy Goan, Westbrook, ME

Acknowledgments (cont.)

Nicole Bess, Spokane, WA
Norine Roberts, Spokane, WA
Peggy Barnes, Atlanta, GA
Rita Walden, Aiken, SC
Stacy Winterfeld, Seattle, WA
Sunie Caballero, Spokane, WA

Lesley University Faculty

Berta Berriz, Ed.D.
Francine Jennings, Ed.D.
Prilly Sanville, Ph.D.
Robert Shreefter, M.F.A.
Sally Rogers, M.Ed.
Susan Griss, M.A.
Vivian Poey, M.F.A.

Collaborators

Kerrie Bellisario, M.F.A., has been working in the arts, education, and cultural heritage arenas for nearly two decades. She is an educational researcher and teaches art culture and community and visual arts integration in Lesley University's Integrated Teaching through the Arts program. She was formerly Associate Director in Lesley University's Creative Arts in Learning Division where she co-founded the graduate program Masters of Education in Arts, Community, and Education. She also served as Executive Director of ArtWorks!, Partners for the Arts and Community, Inc. in New Bedford, MA, where she ran an inner-city teen arts center, creating numerous arts educational programs for youth ages Pre-K–21. She is currently an independent consultant, working with several clients, including most recently Lesley University, the National Park Service, and Crayola™.

Maureen Creegan Quinquis, M.F.A., is a core faculty member at Lesley University and the Director of the Visual Arts Education program in the Creative Arts in Learning Division. She received a Master of Fine Arts degree from the Tufts University/Boston Museum School program, and a Masters of Education from Endicott College in the Arts and Learning program. Maureen is currently completing her doctorate degree in Interdisciplinary Education Studies. Maureen's research interests include visual ethnography and the qualitative research processes at work in the creation of artworks in professional art schools.

Susan J. Fisher, M.Ed., is a visual artist, ceramic sculptor, calligrapher, and photographer, and exhibits regularly. She combines her love of art history and creating art with her educational philosophy. For over 30 years she has approached life both as an artist and educator. She is national faculty for Lesley University's Creative Arts in Learning Masters Education program and is on the faculty at Clark University and Worcester State College. She has been teaching for Lesley University for 22 years. When teaching, she tries to encourage students to find their voices through the arts and the creative process.

Priscilla Harmel, M.Ed., is national faculty for the Creative Arts in Learning Division in the Integrated Teaching Through the Arts Program at Lesley University. She teaches several courses both on and off campus. She is a registered dance therapist and works at the Community Therapeutic Day School in Lexington, MA, and is a teaching artist for Very Special Arts (VSA) of Massachusetts. She has taught internationally in Peru, Brazil, Israel, and India, and nationally throughout the United States. She has been a consultant and curriculum writer on Autism Spectrum Disorder for Understanding Our Differences in Newton, MA, and was a contributor to The Multi-Arts Resource Guide for VSA of Massachusetts. Priscilla collaborated with Preservation Worcester and her work was filmed for a training video on Architecture in Movement for the Head Start program in Worcester, MA.

 **Mary Clare Powell** is a poet (three volumes) and writer of books and articles about the arts and education (*The Arts, Education and Social Change*). Partially retired from Lesley University, she has done research on the arts in schools in western Massachusetts and is on the Steering Committee of Franklin County Arts and Culture to promote artists in Franklin County, MA. She also sits on the Board of Trustees of Pioneer Valley Performing Arts Charter Public School in South Hadley, MA. Through teaching poetry for Lesley University, she continues her work with teachers all across the country, helping them enter the world of poetry for themselves and their students.

 **Margaret (Meg) Lippert, Ed.D.**, has been a professional storyteller for four decades and is the author of 22 award-winning books of multicultural folk tales, including four co-authored with Liberian storyteller Won-Ldy Paye: *Why Leopard Has Spots, Head Body Legs, Mrs. Chicken and The Hungry Crocodile*, and *The Talking Vegetables*. A former classroom teacher and professor of children's literature at Teachers College Columbia University, she is a national faculty member at Lesley University, where she teaches storytelling and is the storytelling mentor for 11 storytelling instructors. Her website, www.StoryPower.net, describes her storytelling performances and workshops.

 **Celeste Miller, M.F.A.**, is a choreographer, teaching artist, and educator. She teaches creative movement in Lesley University's Integrated Teaching Through the Arts Masters in Education program. Her methodologies for dance-arts integration in the K–12 classroom have developed primarily through 18 years of work as founding co-director of Jacob's Pillow Dance Festival Curriculum in Motion. She uses these techniques in school residencies across the United States, working with students, classroom teachers, and teaching artists. Miller holds a Masters in Fine Arts in Dance from Hollins University/American Dance Festival. Currently she teaches in the Department of Theatre and Dance at Grinnell College in Iowa.

 **Kristina Lamour Sansone, M.F.A.**, bridges graphic design and Pre-K–12 education. Her passion for this work stems from personal struggles in text-heavy high school environments, and the educational liberation she found in design. For the past 20 years, Kristina has consulted for schools in New Haven, San Francisco, Austin, and Boston. She is currently on the design team for a new Boston public school that will incorporate graphic design and Universal Design for Learning into all aspects of the curriculum.

Introduction

Arts Integration: The Ripple Effect

What happens when the arts are integrated into the curriculum? What effect, if any, does integrating the arts have on students? teachers? curriculum? learning? the classroom and school community? How do the arts support the Common Core and state standards? The intention of this book is to explore these questions and dive deeper into the theory and practice of what it means to truly and authentically integrate the arts.

Imagine a still pool of water. A pebble, when dropped into the middle, splashes quietly. Slowly the ripples emerge and travel outward in expanding circles. It becomes clear that the consequence of the seemingly simple initial event, the dropping of the stone, goes far beyond the place where it started. The impact is far reaching. There is not only a surface ripple effect, but also a ripple effect that is felt far beneath the surface.

Teachers enrolled in an M.Ed. Integrated Teaching through the Arts (ITA) program with Lesley University were assigned the task of creating a metaphor or simile that accurately demonstrated the power of arts integration. They were asked to somehow demonstrate what happens when the arts are infused into the curriculum as a learning and assessment tool.

Having experienced the arts themselves and with their students over a period of several months, each group of teachers came up with amazingly creative solutions. One group thought of the arts as transformative—like yeast in bread dough or the startling change of moving from a black and white photo to color. Others thought it was like tending a garden or traveling to unknown places. The solutions were creative and meaningful, each illustrating how the arts transform, nurture, change things at a deeper level, and allow for multiple perspectives and multiple voices to be heard and honored.

One group of five students created the metaphor of the ripple effect. They demonstrated this by filling a kiddie pool with water and then throwing in about 20 corks, which bobbed around, seemingly without any particular direction or relationship to one another. We all quietly stood over the pool, watching the corks. They seem to float aimlessly in the water. Then someone dropped one stone right in the middle of the pool. Everything immediately changed. The stone, having broken the surface, immediately disrupted the quiet pool and the bobbing corks. As the ripples began to spread, one circle multiplied into another, and then another (Shafak 2010).

We stood in awe as we watched the corks, no longer meaninglessly floating about, but moving, connecting, creating patterns, and working in synchronization. What became quickly apparent was that the total effect of the dropped stone was not immediately evident. The consequences went much deeper than what was witnessed on the surface. As we continued to observe the ripples, the connections between the ripple effect and integrating the arts became more and more evident and more profound.

What Is Arts Integration?

Arts integration is the investigation of curricular content through artistic explorations. In this process, the arts provide an avenue for rigorous investigation, representation, expression, and reflection of both curricular content and the art form itself.

—Diaz, Donovan, and Pascale (2006)

For many educators, although the idea of integrating the arts seems somewhat appealing, the challenge of having to be "comfortable" in every art form seems overwhelming. "I can't do it," is a familiar response. "I'm not an artist. I can't draw. And for heaven's sake, don't ask me to sing!"

It is important to remember that integrating the arts is not about creating professional artists. It is about deepening learning and about reaching all students of every ability, ethnicity, and linguistic background. It is most definitely about teaching students who learn in a variety of ways, not just through reading and writing.

Another misconception about arts integration is that if we integrate the arts, we risk eliminating the art and music specialists. Nothing is further from the truth. We need both! The specialists focus on teaching the specific skills and elements of a particular art form. In the classroom, the arts are a vehicle for strengthening the core curriculum, and deepening and assessing learning. When the arts are integrated, learning is experienced in a variety of ways, allowing every student to be successful in various content areas.

Several prominent educational leaders in the country, such as Jonathan Kozol, Deborah Meier, Nel Noddings, Linda Darling Hammond, Maxine Greene, and Elliott Eisner, have spoken out against the narrowness of current curriculum, and have expressed the need to reform our educational system and nurture students to become creators, meaning-makers, and empathizers (Pink 2005). It was John Dewey (1931) who remarked that the problem is "with our lack of imagination in generating leading ideas. Because we are afraid of speculative ideas, we do, and do over and over again, an immense amount of specialized work in the region of 'facts.' We forget such facts are only data... uncompleted meanings, and unless they are rounded out into complete ideas—a work which can only be done by...a free imagination of intellectual possibilities—they are as helpless as are all maimed things."

The arts provide an educational approach that addresses these concerns by engaging students in their learning, developing curriculum where curiosity is central and where students tap into their creativity while developing the skills needed for the 21st century, including creativity, collaboration, critical thinking, and communication. The corks, whether you think of them as curriculum content, individual students, or the entire classroom, no longer bob around aimlessly and in isolation, but react, respond, and interact.

When students learn about cells or molecules by actually "becoming" a molecule through a movement exercise as a way to internalize and personalize the understanding, or by writing a persona poem about who they are, what they do, and how they think and feel as a lung or blood cell, or by dramatizing, through a tableau experience, the meaning of the word "metamorphosis," deep learning occurs. It goes way beyond the "right answer." Learning sticks and is meaningful and relevant. They are indeed mastering 21st century skills—creativity, critical thinking, communication, and collaboration—that are essential for higher-order thinking.

As Silverstein and Layne (2010) note, "Arts integration provides multiple ways for students to make sense of what they learn (construct understanding) and makes their learning visible (demonstrate understanding). It goes beyond the initial step of helping students learn and recall information to challenging students to take the information and facts they have learned and do something with them to build deeper understanding."

The Arts Are Not an Extra

A second grade teacher writes about the difficulty of finding space for the arts in her curriculum even though she knows it is an effective tool to enhance learning for her students. She says, "Our district is currently using a prescribed basal program utilizing specific stories. We have little freedom or time to work or think outside the mandated box. Our students, as well as ourselves, have less opportunity to create and use imagination beyond the curriculum that everyone hears at the same time and in the same way."

Her dilemma is one that many educators across the country are facing. However, if we truly want children to learn, we have little choice but to include ways to teach that reach the diverse learners who make up today's classrooms. It is not about "fitting" the arts into the curriculum, but weaving them into the curriculum as a natural part of how the content is presented and assessed. The arts must be thought of as a foundation, the supporting structure that carries the importance of learning.

Jonathon Kozol (2007) worries that artistry and imaginative creativity on the part of teachers is under serious assault. According to Kozol, "The over-determined lesson plans now commonly in use in inner-city neighborhoods, which are often written word for word from scripted programs that are handed to the teachers and intended to keep children on an absolutely straight line to the destination of the next high stakes exam, leave little time for teachers to pay close attention to those children who won't give the answers we are told we must elicit from them or who, even more unpardonably, ignore our pre-planned questions and insist on asking better questions of their own" (50).

The arts are central to human learning and can serve as a foundation for education in many different settings. We live in a wonderfully culturally diverse society. By practicing culturally responsive education we acknowledge, affirm, and celebrate diversity through many lenses, including differences in learning styles, age, class, levels of mental and physical ability, gender, race, and ethnicity. Modeling understanding of differences in our teaching and examining with students the richness and the challenges of a diverse society is essential. "Learning to look through multiple perspectives, young people may be helped to build bridges among themselves; attending to a range of human stories, they may be provoked to heal and transform" (Greene 1992).

The arts provide a variety of ways for students to use what scientists and mathematicians refer to as *representational fluency* —the ability to use different symbolic systems to represent meaning. A concept that grew out of science and math disciplines, representational fluency "includes visualizing and conceptualizing transformation processes abstractly…transforming physical sensory data into symbolic representations and vice versa" (Lesh and Doerr 2003, 288). The arts provide opportunities for students to move between different representations of content. For students to create arts-based work, they must translate their understanding of content into new forms. They cannot translate without understanding. In order to move between languages and symbol systems to create new representations, students must draw upon higher-order critical thinking skills such as analysis and evaluation, leading to artistic creation. In poetry, students use words in new ways that are fresh and derive new meaning; in drama, they explore ideas through character, dramatic context, and multiple perspectives. Visual art harnesses the power of metaphor, and movement boils concepts down into their essence in ways that defy literal interpretation. Students translate information into new forms, blending ideas with their own unique perspectives, background experiences, voice, and intent.

Research continues to show how the arts are not mere window-dressing in the public school setting, but rather that when integrated properly into a curriculum, they can increase learning in key content areas. In a Ford-funded research study, *Voices from the Field: Investigating Teachers' Perspectives on the Relevance of Arts Integration in Their Classrooms* (Bellisario and Donovan with Prendergast 2012), teachers were asked what benefits they discovered from arts integration practices in their classrooms. The data suggests that arts integrated teaching:

- leads to deep learning and increased student engagement.

- provides a variety of strategies for assessing content and expressing understanding.

- is culturally responsive and creates learning that is relevant in students' lives.

- engages students in creativity, innovation, and imagination.

- renews teachers' commitment to teaching.

Why should the arts be an integral part of teaching and learning?

- The arts address multiple learning styles, recognize multiple intelligences, and reach across cultures and languages to address the needs of every student.

- The arts promote analytical and critical thinking skills and can be used to motivate learning and assess it.

- The arts address diversity by helping teachers create classrooms that teach to the needs of every student by presenting multiple perspectives, engaging parents and communities in learning, helping teachers critique schools as institutions, and instituting education reform.

- The arts promote more democratic classrooms by expanding the number of languages able to be used in learning and by encouraging multiple perspectives.

In the Classroom

Katie Palmer, fifth grade teacher in Coeur d'Alene, Idaho, reports that "only 20 students out of 63 received A grades on last year's science test on plant and animal cells. This year, I integrated music and poetry throughout the science unit, and 40 out of 63 got As. They really nailed it this year thanks to the arts!"

Addressing 21st Century Skills Through the Arts

Educators and schools continue to face tough educational challenges. Amid the pressure to raise test scores, lower dropout rates, increase cognitive outcomes, and decrease disciplinary issues while effectively teaching to a wide range of abilities and ethnicities, there is increasing concern about how to best prepare today's students for success in a creative global economy.

There is a set of life and career skills and knowledge that most educators would agree are required in order for students to succeed:

- They must think critically and creatively.

- They must have organizational skills.

- They must be able to work well with others.

- They need to be self-confident, self-motivated, and self-disciplined.

- They need to understand and use mathematics, science, and technology.

- They need to be highly effective communicators.

- They need to understand and appreciate cultural diversity.

James Bau Graves notes that, "The new imperative is creativity. We don't need our schools to inculcate the habits of menial labor; the new economy needs a workforce that is trained in creativity. And that fundamentally implies a new and unprecedented attention to the arts" (2005, 129).

The practice of arts integration has proven to help students understand and practice these important skills. Arts integration employs strategies that build a strong platform for deep and meaningful learning. Students do not merely acquire information, but process and apply it. Observing, recording and organizing, collaborating, planning, practicing, revisiting, making predictions, experimenting, and communicating are among the life and career skills that are enhanced through arts integration (Burdette 2011). This is the kind of deep learning that students will need in the future. "More than ever, their health and well-being, success in the workplace, ability to construct identities and thrive in a pluralistic society, as well as their sense of agency as active citizens depends on gaining these skills" (Dunleavy and Milton 2008, 4).

Addressing Differentiation Through the Arts

Through differentiated instruction, teachers use varied strategies, resources, materials, and procedures to ensure that all students access curriculum and achieve learning goals. This includes providing scaffolds for struggling students while at the same time challenging advanced students. "All students, from the most struggling to the most advanced, need to have curricula that lead to the enduring understandings, essential knowledge, and fundamental skills that are at the heart of the unit of study" (Conklin 2009).

There is also distinct evidence that differentiating instruction through the arts has a unique ability to reach children who might otherwise be left behind by academics. In 1999, the President's Committee on the Arts and Humanities released a study, *Champions of Change: The Impact of the Arts on Learning*, which shows that young people with arts-rich experiences achieved higher grades in school and scored better on standardized tests across all subject areas, including non-arts subjects. Achievement gains were most significant for youths from multicultural and low-income backgrounds—communities that are too often underserved. The arts have the power to engage youth in positive learning and personal growth (Fiske 1999).

By integrating the arts with content instruction, teachers can effectively differentiate to ensure that all learners reach chosen learning goals. The arts embody many paths to learning and inherently encompass multiple modalities through which students can show what they know. For example, kinesthetic learning is an essential aspect of creative movement, drama, and storytelling. The visual learning modality is engaged not only through the visual arts, but also through gesture in storytelling and tableaux in drama. The auditory modality is used not only in music, but also in storytelling, drama, and poetry.

In the same way, multiple intelligences are also engaged when students learn content through the arts (Gardner 1983). For example, music not only utilizes musical intelligence, but also logical-mathematical intelligence through rhythm and pattern and bodily-kinesthetic intelligence through singing or playing rhythm and melody. Drama engages spatial, linguistic, interpersonal, and bodily-kinesthetic intelligences. The visual arts can employ spatial, logical-mathematical, intrapersonal, and even naturalistic intelligences.

Arts integration can also provide open-ended assignments, vocabulary development, self-paced activities, "sense-making" activities, and choice-based activities driven by student interest, all key strategies for differentiated instruction. For example, presenting an array of art-making supplies and encouraging students to think critically about which materials they will use to create a visual arts piece requires students to use critical thinking skills and provides opportunity for student choice. Working with English language learners to create a song about science content is an open-ended task that bolsters vocabulary development and helps students make sense of the curricular material.

To truly differentiate instruction for all learners, teachers must continually assess student progress and understanding and adjust instruction accordingly. The arts provide flexible ways for students to demonstrate their knowledge at various stages of the learning process. For example, when students improvise scenes about mathematics content at the beginning of a unit of study, they demonstrate their prior knowledge of the content. The teacher can then plan instruction to meet students' needs based on the information learned through the scenes. The same improvisational activity performed during the course of the unit can be seen by both students and teacher as a formative assessment, showing what students have learned and demonstrating continued gaps in knowledge. Further instruction can then be adjusted to address student needs. When the dramatic activity is completed at the end of the unit, it can serve as a summative, performance-based assessment to show everything students have learned about the content.

The arts provide multiple, varied, open-ended ways for students to show what they have learned. A range of languages and symbol systems is available to students outside of the written expression students are expected to use in writing essays and taking tests. In the visual arts, an endless array of materials can be used to create pieces, in both 2D and 3D formats, and students can use line, color, texture, shape, and all the languages of visual art to show what they know about content. Pitch, tone, rhythm, and melody in music can be used to represent learning through voices, instruments, or simply clapping. Every student's product will be different. Students understand, through rubrics, checklists, and formative feedback, what they are expected to show they have learned, but there is no one "right" answer.

In the Classroom

Elementary teacher Sunie Caballero reports, "After nine years of teaching in the same elementary school that I attended as a child, I was beginning to feel bored.... Every day, I felt like a reading drill sergeant. I would faithfully administer 90 minutes of reading instruction plus an additional 30–90 minutes of interventions for the poor kiddos who were not reading at the expected level. Once I would suffer through the reading, I would then cram in 90 minutes of math instruction and if possible throw in some science, social studies, and writing. I would try to make my lesson plans creative and enriching, but I was frustrated, and so were my kids."

Sunie discovered that by integrating the arts, every student's strengths were accentuated and even her least productive students proved to be more successful. She had students use the reading material to create their own stories and illustrate them (storytelling and visual arts), create short improvisational skits based on the reading texts (drama), and make up songs and chants to summarize key facts (music and poetry). The curriculum was presented in a way that was innovative and interesting because it engaged many different learning styles, and to her delight, Sunie found she was much more easily addressing the Core Curriculum goals and state standards. Neither she nor her students were bored and behavioral management issues decreased! In fact, the students looked forward to reading time because they were personally engaged.

How to Use This Book

We suggest that you begin to read this book wherever you feel comfortable. Pick a chapter that you are curious about or that resonates with you, or read the book cover to cover. The book begins with investigations of six art forms: poetry, storytelling, music, drama, creative movement, and visual arts. In these chapters, basic information is presented about the specific elements of each art form, and assumptions and perceptions are investigated. Following that, there are specific examples and ideas for integrating the arts in the curriculum for grades K–12. Throughout these chapters, *In the Classroom* sections feature the voices of teachers who successfully integrated the arts into their classrooms. The final chapter shows you the nuts and bolts of creating a unit of study using arts integration.

Let this book work for you. Open it up and dive in. In the spirit of the stone dropped in the water, we hope you will begin by dropping even a small pebble into your classroom pool. Observe what happens. Even if your stone is miniscule in size and the ripples that form are indeterminable waves, something is happening, and that something will continue to grow and expand and deepen. The learning environment is changing not only on the surface, but underneath as well. Transformation is inevitable.

Pay attention. Particularly notice the student who, up until now, is currently not connecting, who struggles to understand content, or who can't sit still long enough to take it all in. Notice the students who always succeed, no matter what. How has integrating the arts challenged each of them? Are they doing more than simply successfully regurgitating information to pass the test? Is learning deepened through imagination and innovation? What has happened to the classroom environment? Is behavioral management less of an issue? Why?

Notice your own energy around teaching. What happens to you as a teacher when you integrate the arts in your unit on Westward Expansion, weather, or Shakespeare? What shifts for you when you allow students to become the creators, the inventors? How does your role change? Notice what happens in assessment. Are there improved results? Are students retaining information and becoming more successful? Has their confidence level risen?

Airplane flight attendants often remind us that we should put on our oxygen masks first before helping others. However, as educators, sometimes we find this the most difficult challenge of all. It is easy to leave the needs of the teacher behind, administering everything possible to support our children. And thus, what is often overlooked is the impact integrating the arts has on teachers and teacher creativity.

"The arts can feed the inner lives of teachers, and the whole education enterprise depends on the quality of those inner lives... Creativity involves drawing on sources from within, finding images, words, sounds, or movement inside oneself to express one's perceptions. This is what artists do. When teachers begin creating in the arts, they do the same.... They come to trust themselves as facilitators for children's learning and become powerful catalysts to evoke children's creativity" (Powell 1997). For both teachers and students, the arts have the power to renew energy, transform classrooms, and create innovative curriculum that inspires everyone to become life-long learners.

If we really want students to not just learn for the test but to also be inspired, life-long learners, we must create opportunities for learning to take place in an environment that allows for reflection, wonder, and creativity. "It is, in fact, nothing short of a miracle that the modern methods of instruction have not entirely strangled the holy curiosity of inquiry" (Einstein quoted in Noddings 2006, 168). Our students deserve every opportunity possible to become curious, imaginative, inspired learners. Drop the stone. Watch what happens.

Chapter 1

Exploring the Language of Poetry

What Is Poetry?

Poetry is a unique use of language. Merryl Goldberg, in her latest edition of *Arts Integration*, suggests that poetry is "a playing with words" (Goldberg 2012). Poetry suggests rather than tells. It accentuates metaphor and image. Emily Dickenson captures the essence of poetry so beautifully in the first line of her poem "Tell all the Truth but tell it slant—" (Johnson 1960). That's what poetry allows us to do—to use language with a bit of freedom; to put words together without worrying about rules of grammar and punctuation. "Poetry is a language organized, produced, and experienced as an art form. If someone believes something is poetry, then, as far as I'm concerned, it is poetry" (Morice 1995).

Poetry provides children with a way to perceive the world, to see things in great detail and through all the senses. It's about paying attention, observing, being awake in the moment, looking for sights, sounds, smells, feelings, and more. It's a way of playing with language, using image, repetition, pattern, sound, metaphor, and mood. When approached creatively, the result is a passion for writing and listening to poetry. Poetry can provide students a taste of freedom and pleasure with language.

Why Does Poetry Matter?

Including poetry as an integral part of education can engage students and help them bring together critical thinking and reflection. Listening to beautiful language filled with poetic images captures children's imaginations and deepens the intricacies of language such as metaphor, simile, and sound patterns created by alliteration. Poetry gives teachers authentic text in which to work on phonics, phonemic awareness, fluency, comprehension, writing, and language development skills such as rhyme, word families, and alliteration (Gill 2007; Perfect 1999; Whitin 1982; Common Core State Standards Initiative 2010). Poems provide a simpler context for students to practice these skills, using text that is at their interest and academic levels (Stickling, Prasum, and Olsen 2011). Writing poetry temporarily frees students from some of the conventions of writing, which they often find restrictive, and allows them to focus on theme, word choice, and the music of language.

Poetry is a powerful tool to expand content learning beyond the language arts as well. In social studies, reading poetry can bring students to the heart and soul of the culture or era being studied. The rhythm and pattern in poetry are certainly mathematical. And creating poetry about science and mathematics helps students create mental images and forge new understanding.

Poetry in the Common Core State Standards

Poetry is a genre that naturally and inherently addresses the Common Core State Standards in language arts. Describe, analyze, narrate, explain, listen, speak, write using alliteration, metaphor; these are all skills found in the ELA and Common Core State Standards that are beautifully addressed through poetry. Reading, writing, and understanding poetry are an integral part of the standards for reading, as well as speaking and listening. Poetry is specifically listed as one of three text types of literature students should read, and skills related to poetry are woven through the standards. For example, students are expected to understand figurative language, word relationships, and nuanced meanings (Grade 8), analyze the impact of rhymes and other repetitions of sound (Grade 7), and create audio recordings of poems that demonstrate fluid reading (Grade 3). Although poetry is not among the genres of writing specified in the Common Core State Standards, it provides students an opportunity to apply what they have learned about language through their reading of poetry. Through poetry, teachers can address many Common Core State Standards related to phonics, phonemic awareness, language development, fluency, comprehension, word recognition, vocabulary development, use of metaphor and simile, and imagery.

In addition to strengthening content learning, poetry in the classroom has positive emotional and social effects on students. Through reading and writing poetry, children are free to take risks and express their deep feelings that precede critical analysis.

A high school English teacher in California used poetry with a group of students who struggled with low achievement and low self-esteem. She sensed that perhaps using this strategy might interest them. She began by first reading her own *I Am From* poem (see page 41 for more information). Aware of her students' difficult life situations, she explained that it was not necessary to share every detail of their lives, and in fact, she had carefully decided what to put in her own poem and what details to leave out. She gave her students some topics to explore such as home, memories, neighborhood, particular sayings they remember, or special places. She urged them to bring in details—sights, sounds, smells, etc.

Once the class began working on the assignment, she became aware that one student, who had struggled all year and spent most of his time unengaged and uninterested, was writing with fervor. When he finished, he raced to her desk and asked if he could go to the computer lab and type up his poem. The teacher was astounded. It was the first time he had actually written anything of substance. He returned and proudly turned in an extraordinary poem. The following is an excerpt from his poem:

> I am from the city of God, the land of lords, the foothill of life, the lights of the moon and stars. I am from the city of racism. I am from the land of freedom.
>
> I am from the piss in the hallway. I am from the streets, the cold hard streets.
>
> I am from the land where people die on corners. I am from the land that everybody wants to live in but where I will die in.
>
> I am from the city where you have to watch your back. I am from the land that never dies. I am from a place where they told me I would never make it; never finish. I am from the ghetto and I will make it!

—High school student, California, 2007

For this particular student, and for many students, writing a poem touches something deep inside. Poetry gave this student a vehicle for expression, voicing the intense frustration and pent-up emotions that hitherto he had left unsaid. His voice, up until that moment, was rarely heard. This poetry exercise opened a door that had previously been closed.

Many teachers had given up on this student: "He can't do anything. Just let him be." He intuitively knows that and reiterates those beliefs in his poem: "I am from a place where they told me I would never make it; never finish." Through the vehicle of poetry, a conversation about what was possible began. It allowed his teacher and others who worked with him to view him in terms of possibility and success instead of only failure. Poetry, like the other art forms, not only gives students a powerful voice but also allows students to be successful in ways that, through conventional educational strategies, seemed impossible.

Bring Poetry into Your Life

Many of us read the newspaper daily, peruse magazines, enjoy novels, and dive into nonfiction work with gusto. But how many of us read poetry on a regular basis? Not many, I'd guess. Why not? What has stopped us? Is it too hard? Too complicated? Not accessible? Just too much work to figure out? Perhaps poetry holds unpleasant memories from school when we were required to dissect a poem with such doggedness that it lost all meaning. Now any enjoyment the reading of poetry held for us in the past has disappeared.

On the other hand, I suspect there are large numbers of us who have pleasant memories of chanting jump rope rhymes, nursery rhymes, table graces, nighttime prayers, and a number of other poetic pieces that we can still happily rattle off today, years later. These poetic verses were fun to learn and continue to be a joy to recite. What is the difference? Perhaps it is the love of poetry, the sheer pleasure in the sounds, rhythms, words, and images.

Many teachers avoid poetry, dread teaching it, do not think of themselves as poets, and thus miss the opportunity to use it as an essential teaching strategy. Kenneth Koch (1999), author of the magical book of children's poetry *Wishes, Lies and Dreams: Teaching Children to Write Poetry*, has taught poetry in New York public schools for years, and feels that children are not given the exposure to valuable writing because teachers are intimidated by it and have the false impression that children are unable to respond to poetry—that it is "too difficult" or too stylized for children to comprehend, never mind articulate on. In fact, Koch's examples of children's poetic writing affirms their ability to grasp complicated concepts as well as relate such complexities to their own emotions (Poetry Foundation 2012). Teachers, too, can be renewed by poetry and can see that it speaks to their needs, to their yearnings, to their deepest experiences. One of Koch's students sums up why poetry is important: "I like poetry because it puts me in places I like to be" (Koch 2012).

Before introducing poetry in your classroom, it is best to begin by bringing poetry back into your own life. Once you feel comfortable and confident reading and writing poetry, you will be eager to share it with your students. Your enthusiasm and experience will transfer to the students, and the students, too, will find similar joy. Step one is to overcome any preconceptions long held about what poetry really is or what it means to write poetry or be a poet.

Read Poetry

Begin by reading and enjoying poetry yourself. Go to a bookstore or a library and browse contemporary poetry books. See what touches you. Find poems that you like, that please you. You'll soon discover that there are poets with whom you resonate, who seem to describe experiences like you might have had. If there are poems you like, bring them to class and read them to your students. Avoid teaching about form; don't try to analyze them, just read them aloud. Poetry can be a presence in a classroom, without any interpretation, without any commentary. Simply make a place for poetry. Enjoy the process.

Write Poetry

Next, write a poem. Start by drawing a map of the place you grew up. Put everything on it—where the local school was, or church, or your tree house, the park where you hung out, the hill you sledded down. Use this map to connect to your memories. Pick one vivid memory and do a mind map, listing everything you can about that memory. Work through your senses. What sights, sounds, tastes, or smells do you remember? List the details. Who was there? What did it feel like? What was the weather like? What were you wearing? What textures do you remember? What time of day was it? Take the details of this one memory and put it into a loose poetic form. Don't worry about getting it right. Here are a few guidelines to follow as a way to get you started:

- **Don't try to rhyme.** Most contemporary poems don't rhyme. Rhyme is traditionally part of constructing a poem, but let it emerge on its own, and not at the end of lines. Reading poetry out loud to yourself is a good way to hear the rhythm and the rhyme or near rhyme. You might discover that writing poetry is easier and provides much more freedom if you are not saddled with trying to find a rhyming word.

- **Write in phrases, not full sentences.** You are creating impressions, details, and suggestions of meaning. This is part of the joy of breaking out of standard English syntax and diction. Write in fragments or phrases.

- **Show, don't tell.** Use sensory words. Give an impression of what happened. Bring it to life through emotions and through all the senses. Resist telling the reader what to think or how to interpret what you are saying. There is no need to point to the obvious. Play around. The heart of a poem lies in its images—word pictures that the poet paints in order to recreate a scene, an experience, a memory, etc. Images are drawn from the senses—seeing, hearing, smelling, tasting, touching. Poetry is grounded in the tangible world. Using images enables your poetry to *show* what you are writing about, rather than *telling* or summarizing it.

- **Use ordinary language.** Poetry does not require fancy words. The words you use to speak with are strong and will be equally so when you write them down. There is no one to impress. Don't worry about coming up with "poetic words." They don't exist. Choose every word because it is the best, freshest, least clichéd word you can think of.

- **Use metaphor to compare two things.** Writing using metaphor is an attempt to condense language and vividly connect two unlike things together, making a startling juxtaposition, such as *My words are kites*. A metaphor (or simile, using *like* or *as*, which is weaker than a more direct comparison) helps your poetry to "leap," that is, to move from one category of thought to another, to easily and powerfully summarize how one thing resembles another, and thus to illuminate the first idea with an economy of words. Metaphors are powerful, and metaphorical thinking is a higher-order thinking skill; it takes some practice.

- **Read your poem aloud to yourself to hear its rhythm.** Rhythm exists naturally in language and most of us are delighted by it. Line breaks can help create a rhythm that supports the meaning of the words you are writing and fosters complex and pleasant thought.

Once you have something on paper, go back and revisit it again and again. Work with it. Edit it. Put it away and get it out again...and again. If you can, read it to someone else and have that person help you revise it.

And finally, share it! Poetry is meant to be read aloud. Honor it by giving it an audience. The final step is to give it away. In this way you complete the writer/reader connection that happens in all art forms, the sharing of the created piece. Poems make delicious gifts.

Introduce Poetry to Your Students

Once you have experienced the power of poetry for yourself, you will be excited to share it with your students. Begin by reading poetry to students and having them read it to each other. United States Poet Laureate Pat Lowerey Collins argues that reading poetry develops some fundamental cognitive and intellectual skills, and that reading a poem "replicates the way we learn and think" (quoted in Showalter 2012, 63). He sees many parallels between poetry and learning: "When we read a poem, we enter the consciousness of another. It requires that we loosen some of our fixed notions in order to accommodate another point of view…. To follow the connections in a metaphor is to make a mental leap, to exercise an imaginative agility, even to open a new synapse as two disparate things are linked." Collins considers poetic form as "a way of thinking, an angle of approach" that helps students understand how information must be "shaped and contoured in order to be intelligible."

The best way to introduce poetry to students is to have them listen to poems—all sorts of genres of poetry. Today's students are used to listening to all types of music and they have quite a discerning ear. By listening to poetry, they begin to analyze language and appreciate how meaning is shaped. Listening to a variety of poems also allows them to consider ways in which identity may be perceived and understood as manifested in the poems they hear (Gordon 2009). Ask your students what they remember about the poem they just heard. They are hearing meaning in their own way, through their own ears. What details do they remember? What stuck? Listening to and experiencing poems in sound are important dimensions of engaging with and understanding the meaning potential of texts and the means with which students readily involve themselves.

Our schools are filled with diverse learners and it is important to read a diverse selection of poetry. Integration of culture and the arts into the curriculum for English language learners, and indeed most students, is all too rare. A group of researchers in Canada discovered that poetry was the best practice not only for teaching literacy but also for helping students develop critical thinking and analytical perspectives, and the power of high-interest cultural content motivated language learners beyond all else (Reeves 2009).

Ideally students should read and hear as many poems as possible so they can find their own style of poetry. They should hear traditional poetry as well as contemporary poetry and experience serious and humorous poetry. From this wide variety of poets and poems, students can connect with one or more genres and then move to writing their own poems (Lynch 2009).

As students hear more and more poetry, they hopefully will become more comfortable with it. Assumptions about what poetry is and is not will break down. Just as there is not one genre of music, there is not one genre of poetry. Listening to poems read aloud gives students a chance to feel, think, discover, ask questions, and perhaps get answers. You could begin by simply reading the title and asking students what they think the poem will be about. Ask them to listen to the sounds of the words. Once readers or listeners practice making sense of poetry, they may generalize this useful skill to other texts and genres (Stickling, Prasun, and Olsen 2011).

Figure 1.1 provides some suggested first poems to read aloud to students. Some of these poems have specific forms that can be used by students to model their own writing. It is a good place to help students begin developing their own poetic vocabulary. Musical lyrics can also be analyzed. Bob Dylan's lyrics are often used because of the ingenious way Dylan stresses syllables and plays with metaphor. Figure 1.2 suggests poetry collections for classroom use. See Appendix D: Recommended Resources for more information.

Figure 1.1 Suggested Poems to Read Aloud

Gary Soto	"Oranges"
Emily Dickinson	"Not in Vain"
Seamus Heaney	"Scaffolding"
	"The Rain Stick"
Rudyard Kipling	"If–"
Judith Viorst	"If I Were in Charge of the World"
Kenn Nesbitt	"The Aliens Have Landed"
Jack Prelutsky	"Be Glad Your Nose Is on Your Face"
Langston Hughes	"Dreams"

Figure 1.2 Suggested Poetry Collections

Shel Silverstein	*Where the Sidewalk Ends* (1974)
	A Light in the Attic (1981)
	Falling Up (1996)
Jack Prelutsky	*New Kid on the Block* (1984)
	A Pizza the Size of the Sun (1996)
	Raining Pigs and Noodles (2005)
Betsy Franco	*Messing Around on the Monkey Bars* (2009)
Alan Katz	*Oops!* (2008)
Carol Diggory Shields	*Almost Late to School* (2003)
Sharon Creech	*Hate that Cat* (2008)

Note: Full bibliographic entries for these resources can be found in Appendix D, Recommended Resources.

Once students are comfortable and are enjoying listening to and reading poetry, help them to create their own poems. The following activities will provide enough structure to get students started, but allow for the creativity and expression that makes poetry a rich teaching and learning tool.

Introductory Activity: Poetry About Change

Many curriculum areas include the concept of change. There are seasonal changes, climatic changes, historical changes, changing states of matter, psychological and physical changes, to name just a few. All of these can be transformed into poetic verse! Here is a suggested lesson idea about change, inspired by a personal memory, to use as an introduction to the poetic process.

1. **Warm up:** Start by discussing with students what it means for something or someone to change. With students, brainstorm a list of things that change. The change can be big or small, something that happened quickly, or something that took a long time (e.g., changing homes, changing age, changing friendships, changing hairstyles, changing from riding a tricycle to a two-wheeler, changing an emotion, changing your mind, the change of seasons).

2. **Begin with a memory:** Ask students to try to remember something that changed in their lives. Ask them to visualize where they were when the change happened. What did it feel like? Who was there? What were they wearing? What season was it?

3. **Create a visual picture of the "change memory":** With a range of art materials, have students create a picture of the memory—the place, the happening. The picture does not need to be perfect. It is simply a way to capture the memory visually and bring it to life.

4. **Jot down words and phrases:** Tell students to write down phrases about the change. They should avoid writing complete sentences, but rather bring the change to life through emotions and all the senses. They are trying to *show* the change through images rather than tell about it.

5. **Use metaphor or simile to compare things:** Show students how they can bring the change event to life by showing how one thing resembles another. As a class, brainstorm pairs of words and discuss how they relate to one another. This is a higher-order thinking skill and will be more difficult for younger children, but give it a try! See what happens.

6. **Share the poems:** Have students first read their poems to themselves. Ask them to pay attention to the sound of the poem. Have them ask themselves: Is there anything I want to change? Would other words provide a different rhythm? Can I make it more interesting? Finally, have students read the poems aloud and share them with each other.

Poetry About Change: Curriculum Connections

Once students have created personal change poems, they can create change poems in any content area. Here are some ideas:

- **Social Studies:** Choose a theme from your social studies unit. As a class, think about one aspect of that topic where change has occurred and write a poem about it. For instance, students could write poems about how the adoption of the Constitution changed America, or changes that have occurred in technology over the 20th and 21st centuries.

- **Mathematics:** Numbers change: they increase and decrease; they can be added, divided, and multiplied; they become fractions. Have students write about a mathematical change from the viewpoint of a number.

- **Science:** Have students write about environmental change, perhaps a change from liquid to solid or the change of seasons. In addition to describing the change, they should describe their feelings and attitudes about it. Remind them to be specific and use all their senses in the description.

Poetry Across the Curriculum

Here are some simple poetry activities that can be used at any grade level. Have students create personal poems first so they get the feel for each type of poem, then expand into the content areas.

Word Bowl

A good beginning poetry exercise is the word bowl. It gives you a leg up when facing the blank page and puts participants at ease. It allows for experimentation with words and images. Start by creating a list of words centered on a particular topic. Brainstorm with your students, building a relevant list that includes pronouns, verbs, nouns, prepositional phrases, etc. Find lively words, words that are humorous, attention-grabbing, mesmerizing. Once you have a good long list, write it on paper, then cut the words apart and put them in a large "word bowl."

Have student volunteers reach in (no peeking!) and choose five or ten words from the bowl. Make up a poem together using these words, thinking about the theme or topic you chose. Have students try writing their own poems using these words. Read them out loud and students will see how many poems can come from the same words! Students will quickly get the idea and will be eager to create their own. Word bowls are a great way for students to expand and work with vocabulary in any content area.

"I Am From" Poem

"I am from" poems, developed by George Ella Lyon (2010), allow space for students to share about family traditions, home life, special moments, and memories. In this form, each line begins with the words "I am from," and the poet then relates not only the places, but the emotions, feelings, sights, sounds, smells, and even tastes of his or her life. A wonderful resource and good introduction to this poetic form is *Mama, Where Are You From?* by Marie Bradby (2000).

"I am from" poems invite the stories and voices of your students into the classroom (Christensen 2001). "As we create schools and classrooms that are laboratories for a more just society than the one we now live in, we need to remember to make our students feel significant and cared about."

Try writing your own "I am from" poem first. Going through the process of creating an "I am from" poem and then reading it to your students is an excellent place to begin. It will give the students insight into your life and provide them with a relevant example. You will also be able to talk about your own process of writing the poem. Then, have students create their own "I am from" poems based on their own lives. Here is an excerpt from an "I am from" poem written by a teacher in Idaho:

> I am from an old wringer washer,
> A clothesline full of clothes; crunchy towels, stiff jeans
> And sheets that smell like sunshine.
> I am from homemade bread, hot cereal for breakfast,
> pea soup
> And white, pasty, lima beans.
> I am from canning eternal boxes of fruit and garden
> produce in the summer.
>
> —Liz Thurgood, M.Ed. student, Coeur d'Alene, Idaho

The "I am from" poem carries quite easily into any content area. Have students write "I am from" poems from the point of view of historical figures (social studies), literary characters (language arts), animals (biology), rocks (geology), planets (astronomy), or even geometric solids or graphs (mathematics).

Observation Poem

Have students use all their senses to experience something—a place, a time, an object. Have them note the sizes, shapes, colors, and textures they see, feel, and hear. Ask them to describe the smells and tastes they experience. Then, have them create poems based on these sensory images.

> The pot looks like a pear with a mouth
> The pot's color looks sometimes like the sky
> With wind around it.
> The pot smells like clay with vanilla mixed.
> It feels like a rough rock with a hole.
> It is hollow like a cave.
> I can fit a genie in it.
>
> —Fifth grade student (McKim and Steinbergh 2004, 59)

Observation poems are a great extension to students' recordings of scientific observation. Have them write poems about their experiences observing nature or performing experiments. Just be careful with taste and smell in the lab!

Metaphor Poem

Have students write poems in which they create metaphors for their families: My family is a plate of spaghetti, or a salad, or a box of chocolates. Students should develop the metaphor throughout the poem. Metaphorical thinking is a higher-order thinking skill, and students can't have too much practice in it. Here is an example:

The body is a metropolis

Cell citizens travel vascular highways

Immuno-police chase viral villains

City Hall brain buzzes with communication

Traffic teems through the Town Hall heart

—Eighth grade student

In the content areas, students can write metaphor poems based on historic events ("The Renaissance was a butterfly"), fractals or tessellations ("a Mandelbrot set is a universe"), or anything in the natural world ("a thunderstorm is a temper tantrum," "a rainbow is a celebration").

Persona Poem

Poems from a specific entity's point of view, or *persona poems*, extend the imagination and allow for freedom of voice. In this type of poetry, the writer "becomes" an object or concept and writes about his or her experience. There are objects everywhere, and each holds the potential of becoming the inspiration for a poem—a falling leaf, a burning candle, an archaeological artifact, an historical document, a fractal, a number, a mathematical equation. The excitement for students is to make the connection with their object or concept, get to know it, identify with it...become the object. They should ask themselves questions such as: How do I feel? What do I like best about myself? How do I move? Do I have a special sound or language or smell or taste? Where did I come from? What is my daily life like? What do I believe? How does it feel to be changed into something else?

Below is an example of two persona poems written by fifth graders from Coeur d'Alene, Idaho, as part of their study of plant and animal cells.

I Am a Red Blood Cell

My extravagant red color is ordinary
In this quiet, slippery tube
My nucleus is commanding
"Mitochondria, more ENERGY!"
Because all my parts have important jobs
Sometimes it's tedious
Just flowing and listening
To the only sound anyone can hear.
Breathing
Everyone here is individual
But we are all smooth and round
Which helps us flow effortlessly through this vein
Our animal owner needs us red blood cells
Without us he would die
Then we would have no job
So we would die too
I am a red blood cell

—Fifth grade student, Idaho

The Life of a Nerve Cell

I am a nerve cell.
Wait!
I have a message!
Good thing I am a branching shape.
Wait! Message!
I sent this message already!
I am glad
That I have a good nucleus
Or else I would go crazy!
Wait! Message!
It is already hot in here
And all this work makes it hotter.
My shape helps because the message
can scurry up me.
Like a squirrel up a tree.
Here is another message!
Bye!

—Fifth grade student, Idaho

Age Poem

Have students begin a poem with either "I am in the beginning of my _____ year" or an introductory line that refers to their age. Then, they should write about their life at that point. Tell them to think about games they played, names of friends and teachers, school events, family events, summer pastimes, favorite clothes and foods, etc. This is similar to "I am from" poems but not as commonly done. Age poems prompt students to look at things from a new perspective. Students can create age poems for historical figures, literary characters, or even scientific principles.

Fourteen Year Oxymoron

To be fourteen is to be old and young at the same time. It is a time of clear confusion and happy sadness. It is a dream in reality. Oh! This age! Sane craziness, right wrongness, pleasurable pain. How short and long it is. When I am older I know I will think those were the awfully good times.

—Lown and Steinbergh (1996, 60)

Forms of Poetry

Staring at a blank piece of paper can be daunting to a new poet. When asking students to write poetry, you may want to provide a frame in which to safely create. Here are a few suggestions of forms of poetry to explore.

Acrostic

Acrostic poems are written around a topic word. The topic word is written vertically and each letter begins a line related to the topic.

Ladybugs eat aphids

A ladybug is pretty

Disgusting smells come out when they are scared

Yellow when they come from pupa

Beetles are bugs

Up in the sky flying high

Gardens are where you find them

—Frye, Trathen, and Schlagal (2010)

Cinquain

Cinquain poetry has five lines:

Line 1: 2 syllables

Line 2: 4 syllables

Line 3: 6 syllables

Line 4: 8 syllables

Line 5: 2 syllables

Hide and Seek

You're it!
I'm hiding fast
behind the big oak tree
I'm in a tent of young green leaves
Got you!

—Mary Clare Powell

Plants

I am
a plant, I grow
from a tiny brown seed
I need air, water and sunlight
Flower!

—Mary Clare Powell

Diamante

Diamante poems, or diamond-shaped poems, start with one word on the first line, grow to four words, then go back to one word. The basic structure is:

Line 1: one word—subject/noun that is contrasting to line 7

Line 2: two words—adjectives that describe line 1

Line 3: three words—verbs that relate to line 1

Line 4: four words—nouns: first 2 words relate to line 1, last 2 words relate to line 7

Line 5: three words—action verbs that relate to line 7

Line 6: two words—adjectives that describe line 7

Line 7: one word—subject/noun that is contrasting to line 1

A diamante poem can describe one concept:

Arctic

Arctic

Blustery, desolate

Swirling, screaming, freezing

Caribou, igloos...Camels, tents

Burning, blinding, whistling

Barren, dry

Desert

—Vincent, age 13, Indiana (2008)

A diamante poem can move from one vocabulary word to its antonym:

Morning

Morning
bright, no clouds
stretch, jump up, eat
school and work, play and supper
slow down, rest, relax
cool, dark
evening

—Mary Clare Powell

Or a diamante poem can describe a process:

Caterpillar

Caterpillar
Fuzzy, small
Inching, eating, fattening,
Small, green—colorful, graceful
Cocooning, growing, dreaming
Bright, in flight
Butterfly

—Lovell (2008)

List

List poetry is one of the easiest forms to write. It is made up of a list of items or events and can be any length, rhymed or unrhymed. The topic of a list poem can range from "waiting" to "what bugs me" to any curriculum subject matter. For instance, to reinforce understanding of verbs and prepositions, a list poem could be created in which every line uses a verb or preposition. Any topic can work!

A verb is an action word.

I use verbs every day

I wake up

I eat

I walk

I sing

I read

I study

I run

I sit

I sleep

Concrete

Concrete poems are written so that the placement of the text forms the shape of the subject of the poem. A poem about a triangle would be shaped like a triangle, and a poem about a tree would be shaped like a tree.

Slide

```
        on tightly it is
      as I hold      all
       as long            worth
        but                   it in
         scary                      the
         very                          end
        can be                            because
       ladder                                I get to
      up the                                     whoosh
     going                                           down
```

Haiku

Haiku poetry comes from Japan. Haiku poems have three lines. The first line has five syllables, the second line has seven syllables, and the third line has five syllables. Haiku poems do not rhyme and often the topic is related to nature or the seasons.

Haiku Seasonal Cycle

The lilies open

To announce a new season

Snow rabbits change hue.

The fox finds freedom
Heat waves rise off the moths' wings
The goldfish all swim.

Sharp, crisp winds blowing
Frost forms on the spider web
The animals hide.

The world is white now
Flaky snow from flaky clouds
Look forward to spring.

—Fifth grade student (McKim and Steinberg 2004, 129)

Sharing Poetry

Poems are to be shared. They are to be read to others. Here are a few ways for students to share their poems:

- **Chap books:** A chap book is a pocket-sized book meant for carrying. Collect students' original poems and put them together in a little book. Publish multiple copies to share with parents and with other classes.

- **Poetry cards:** Have students create original poetry greeting cards for special occasions. They can give them to family and friends.

- **Publishing station:** Set up an area in the classroom for students to publish their poetry. Include small booklets, paper, pencils and pens, crayons and markers, decorative stamps, staplers, and tape—whatever students might need to publish their work.

- **Readings:** The music of poetry is best experienced when it is read aloud. Invite parents, administrators, and other classes to a poetry reading where students read their original works aloud to thunderous applause!

Assessment

When designing assessment for arts integration, define the learning goals in both the art form and the content area, and then create assessment tools that reflect these standards and objectives.

- First, determine the poetry objectives. What is the purpose of having students write poetry? Hopefully, one of the first learning goals is not only a proficiency in writing poetry but also a gained love and appreciation for poetry. Do you have expectations of students learning a specific form? Increasing vocabulary? Understanding language complexities such as metaphor, simile, alliteration, personification, mood, pattern, repetition, detail, etc.?

- Once these objectives are determined, create a poetry rubric for assessing students' written work that reflects your learning goals. This rubric can include language arts standards for reading and writing poetry. Speaking and listening goals can be assessed via rubric as students read their poetry aloud. Recording students' readings not only addresses speaking and listening standards, but also makes evaluation easier.

- Define the content area goals as well. How are students expected to show their content area learning through poetry? What vocabulary should be used? What concepts or ideas should be expressed or explained? Integrate these standards and objectives into the poetry rubric, or create a separate rubric to assess content learning.

Here is a sample rubric for a diamante poem in science:

Figure 1.3 Rubric: Solar System Diamante Poems

Assignment: Write a diamante poem about the movements of the planets in our solar system.

Criteria	Advanced	Proficient	Basic
Science standard: Knows characteristics and movement patterns of the planets in our solar system	Uses scientific vocabulary extensively, shows strong understanding of science concept	Uses scientific vocabulary, shows understanding of science concept	Uses little or no scientific vocabulary, does not show understanding of science concept
Poetry standard: Uses strong imagery and interesting word choice	Vivid imagery, strong, interesting, and original word choice	Strong imagery, appropriate word choice	Little imagery, weak word choice
Poetry form	Adheres to all conventions of diamante form	Adheres to most conventions of diamante form	Does not adhere to diamante form
Language Arts standard: Demonstrates understanding of figurative language, word relationships, and nuances in word meanings	Exceeds standard	Meets standard	Falls below standard

Concluding Thoughts

Paul Janeczko confesses in *Reading Poetry in the Middle Grades* that he wishes the culture today was one in which he didn't have to work so hard to convince others that poetry counts (Janeczko 2011). In education today, poetry is often neglected or considered a frill. In an educational environment where schools, teachers, and students are evaluated by test scores, it is easy to push poetry aside and focus on building quantifiable skills.

There is a wonderfully inspiring book, *Teaching with Fire: Poetry that Sustains the Courage to Teach* (Intrator and Scribner 2003), that not only contains powerful poetry, but an introduction to each poem written by a teacher wherein she explains how one particular poem has sustained or helped her reach her students in new ways. Poetry has the power to do that. It can bring meaning not only to our students, but to ourselves as well. "Poetry often gets a bad rap as stodgy and highfalutin. Poet Laureate Billy Collins reminds us to lighten up, and let poetry reach us in things that are human and real" (Intrator and Scribner 2003, 194).

I ask them to take a poem
And hold it up to the light
Like a color slide.
Or press an ear against its hive
I say drop a mouse into a poem
And watch him probe his way out.
Or walk inside the poem's room
And feel the walls for a light switch.
I want them to water-ski
Across the surface of a poem
Waving at the author's name on the shore
But all they want to do

Is tie the poem to a chair with a rope
And torture a confession out of it.
They begin beating it with a hose
To find out what it really means.

—Poet Laureate Billy Collins
(Intrator and Scribner 2003, 194–5)

After reading this chapter on Exploring the Language of Poetry, I hope you are no longer "torturing a poem," but can see that poetry has great value for you and for your students. In 2002, a group of students who participated in a 15-week "Poet in Residence" program, which involved both writing and reading poetry, demonstrated significant achievement in expressive writing, increased vocabulary, and improved critical analysis skills and reading comprehension. And more importantly, during interviews with the students and focus groups following the residency, there was clear indication of an increased positive attitude about writing. Students who were struggling with writing and reading showed marked improvement (Slater 2002).

When students attempt to make sense of a poem, they use critical analysis skills to understand and make meaning. They become sensitive to the mood and sounds of words. When they write their own poetry these skills transfer. Through their own creativity they are able to express their thoughts and feelings. Their voices are heard. Sharing our own voices and listening to others is a gift that must be a part of everyone's educational experience. We owe it to our students and ourselves.

Reflection

1. What is your "poetry attitude" that has been influenced by past poetry experiences?

2. How comfortable are you with using poetry in the classroom?

3. Choose one language arts lesson you plan to teach in the next month. How can you integrate poetry? What content area objectives could you address using poetry? What form of poetry would you use? How would you assess the content learned through poetry?

Chapter 2

Making
Musical
Connections

What Is Music?

Definitions of music often include a list of musical elements, encompassing terms like rhythm, tone, tempo, dynamics, melody, timbre, and pitch. Each of these elements is an integral part of most musical composition, whether instrumental or vocal. But is it possible to have a musical piece that has no clear tone? No melody or pitch? Yes, it is. So what, then, is the most basic definition of music and one that encompasses all music, from all cultures and all genres? Can kicking a chair be music? Does tapping a pencil gently on a desk become a musical composition? The answer, I believe, is *yes*. How can that be possible? What is the distinction between noise and music?

Music is intentional or organized sound (and silence), often using elements such as rhythm, melody, harmony, pitch, etc. If someone bangs randomly on a pile of pots and pans, it makes noise. If they bang on them in a rhythmic way, they are making music. "Stomp Out Loud," a unique musical theatre production featuring choreographed percussion and movement, has revolutionized the idea of what it is to make music. The Stomp performers use ordinary objects like chairs and trash cans, which most of us would never consider "playing" as musical instruments, to create wonderfully engaging compositions. Now that we can consider brooms or keys to be musical instruments, the possibilities are endless.

For those of us who are not familiar with musical terms and do not "read" musical notation, a complicated definition that uses a term such as *timbre* can be off putting. How can I possibly integrate music into my classroom when I can't read music and have no idea what the word *timbre* means? Thinking in terms of music simply being organized sound and silence opens up the possibility for music to be accessible to everyone. It is not only about reading music or analyzing notes, harmony, or melodic lines, although there are many who enjoy doing that. It is about listening and creating sounds and it can also be about creating symbols to represent the sounds, which links directly into literacy because text is a symbolic representation of sound. Musical symbols do not need to be notes on a staff, but rather any representation of a sound that makes sense to the composer or those "reading" the score.

Why Does Music Matter?

Our lives begin with listening to the sound of our mother's heartbeat. Inherent in all of us is a rhythm—our personal rhythm. That rhythm connects us to the greater universe and is directly correlated to learning basic literacy skills. Simple childhood nursery rhymes and singing games are the foundational building blocks that set fluency of language in place. Music is often referred to as the soul of a culture. It connects people, defines who they are, and builds community. Music can inspire us, bring us to tears, calm us, unite us, strengthen us, and connect us with others.

Although often seen as an "extra" in education, music quite naturally addresses key learning standards. Listening, language development, reading, problem solving, and abstract reasoning and patterning can easily be addressed in the curriculum through music integration. English language learner goals, such as developing and expanding modes of expression and communication and developing authentic uses of language, are naturally addressed through music integration, therefore meeting the various needs of all learners in a classroom. Music connects directly to learning language through the use of sound and symbol, reinforcing listening skills, building mathematical concepts of patterning and problem solving, and thinking abstractly.

When teachers and students make music together, they create an atmosphere that celebrates the whole and the individual. More than ever, in an educational environment filled with the pressure of testing and a need to find the "right" answer, our schools today must create places where children feel they belong, places where they discover their own identity, places that honor their approach to learning, and places where they feel ownership of their learning and a connection to the school community.

Common Core

Music in the Common Core State Standards

Musical activities can address Common Core State Standards in both language arts and mathematics. In language arts, students can create lyrics to describe using detail, report on a topic, tell a story, or recount an experience. In some cases they will organize their thoughts and use facts and details to describe, and in others they will paraphrase information. In mathematics, music requires students to reason abstractly and quantitatively, generate and analyze patterns, look for and make use of structure, and attend to precision.

Exploring Perceptions of Music

Music is the predominant art form in public education. A survey by the National Center for Education Statistics (Carey et al. 1995) indicates that some form of music education is offered in 97% of public elementary schools and 94% of public secondary schools (Johnson 2004, 118). Music specialists provide most of this music education. It is the music specialists who play an important role in teaching the technical and performance skills of the art of music.

Music was established in the Boston schools in 1838 and this may be regarded as the initial introductory period of music in schools across the country (Birge 1984). With it came the recognition of music specialists, those who were trained and qualified to teach music. This was beneficial for music specialists, who were finally recognized as worthy additions to a child's education. However, it left the classroom teacher, who previously had included music as part of the basic curriculum, feeling inadequate, and music education would now be left to music specialists—the experts. The result of this shift was, for many children who saw the music specialist only once a week or less, a very limited and narrowly defined experience with music making.

It is no surprise then that many classroom teachers today lack confidence in their musical ability and choose to be engaged in only a very minimal way in musical activities with their students. They feel most comfortable leaving the task of music education to the specialists. If we hope to truly integrate music across the curriculum, ensuring a more comprehensive music and learning experience, the classroom teacher cannot pass the musical baton completely over to the music specialist. To improve teaching and learning through music integration, we must create a multitude of strategies for integrating the arts whereby every educator, both music specialist and classroom teacher, plays an active part. Everyone must be engaged in music making at some level.

Music education is often considered as a separate subject and not usually integrated into the classroom curriculum. Our perception of music making, beginning with singing, is often narrowly defined and in most cases continues to be considered, by most educators, to require a great deal of training involving learning complicated skills in breathing, vocal technique, diction, and note reading (Pascale 2005). Many classroom teachers feel that they are not proficient enough at singing to teach music in their classrooms. They are happy to put on a CD in the background, but sing? Oh…no, leave that to the music specialist. It is difficult to convince many teachers otherwise.

In researching the cultural idea of "singers" and "non-singers," the collected data suggested that, in fact, the categories themselves are a cultural phenomenon (Pascale 2002). Western culture has created the category "singer." And thus, by default, a "non-singer" category was created. In order to qualify as a singer, according to the research, you must, among many things, have confidence, be outgoing, musically expressive, and vocally talented, have a large repertoire of songs, sing in tune, and have a good, strong voice.

This notion of only some people being singers is a Western cultural phenomenon and not universal. In Ghana, for example, the distinction does not exist. "Music," to Ghanaians, is a general term referring to drumming, dancing, and singing, and is integrated into all aspects of life. It functions as a way to bring people together and to convey important cultural, political, and educational messages. Ask a Ghanaian if she is a singer and she looks at you strangely; the question itself makes no sense. Everyone in Ghanaian society is a singer just as everyone is a dancer and drummer. What holds utmost importance in music making to Ghanaians is not how well you sing or drum or dance, but that you participate. Participation, above all else, is essential because music making is about collaboration and relationships (Pascale 2005). As educators, we can take something very important away from this approach.

Bring Music into the Classroom

The challenge for educators is this: Can we embrace this alternative way of thinking about music making? Can we choose to let go of the notion of the non-singer and de-emphasize musical ability, and, in turn, focus on music making as a process that builds community and strengthens learning? It opens the possibility of creating a school environment where everyone is a musician, and everyone is singing. If music in schools is going to continue to flourish and be valued as not only a valuable art form in and of itself, but as an essential learning tool for enhancing curriculum, everyone in the school must participate and be part of the music making.

Part of the paradigm shift is to open our minds to what we even consider music-making to be. For many of us, it means singing, note reading, performing, or mastering an instrument. Let's imagine for a moment that you teach in a school that has a music specialist who the students see weekly. That's great. And there is a weekly morning gathering led by the music specialist that includes singing. Where do you fit, as the classroom teacher? How can you support and enhance your students' music education?

- **Begin by expanding your own perspective of music.** Consider that music making comes in all forms and is not limited to singing or playing a traditional instrument. Think about music making in the broadest sense, as organized sound and silence.

- **Teach students to listen.** With students, explore sound— found sounds, invented sounds, sounds from the environment. Help them pay attention to what they hear and discuss their reactions to sound.

- **Focus on participation, not skill building.** Music in the classroom is about building community or an ensemble of learners and deepening learning of basic curriculum. It is not about teaching note reading and sight singing.

- **Create a safe environment for participation.** Set clear guidelines that allow students (and the teacher!) to participate in music making and singing without judgment. Begin perhaps by singing with a recording, and then once everyone knows the song, turn the recording off. Remember why you are singing—not to select out the "singers," but rather to use songs to enhance curriculum. Everyone in the classroom should be singing. Again, the emphasis is on community, not on whether every voice is exactly in tune. It means a great deal that everyone participates.

Teach Students to Listen

Oddly enough, when suggesting to teachers that the best way to integrate music is to begin with listening, they often give the quizzical response, "That's music?" It is! If we agree that the basic definition of music is organized sound and silence, then paying attention to sounds is an essential ingredient. Begin the process of integrating music by exploring sound and enhancing listening skills.

Just as children's literacy skills are reinforced by being read to, and by hearing stories, children's musical skills are enhanced by listening. And listening, for classroom teachers who feel insecure about music making, is an activity that is accessible and doable and addresses important core content and standards. Listening builds focus, attention span, discrimination, the ability to categorize or skills in categorization, and much more. It is a wonderful way to begin to integrate music.

Most educators spend an inordinate amount of time asking, if not demanding, that children listen. It is quite apparent that many children have stopped listening. They have stopped listening to each other and, usually, have stopped listening to the teacher! And it is no surprise. In today's world we are bombarded with sound. You can rarely walk into a supermarket, mall, airport, railway station, hotel, or any other public space without hearing some kind of "music" or announcement blaring from loud speakers. The sounds of traffic, airplanes, and other people envelop us in our daily lives. And with the advent of technology, many of us are attached to our cell phones, MP3 players, video games, and other devices that add to our soundscape. Not only have children stopped listening, we all have. Given the huge number of sounds that surround us daily, we've made careful choices about what we choose to listen to and what we choose to ignore. Unfortunately, for educators, some children have put us on their "ignore" list!

Open your students' ears, and your own, with active listening. The Listening Walk activity described below is easy to implement, is applicable for any age group, and is adaptable for students with varying abilities. Listening exercises are particularly important to use with students whose first language is not English.

Introductory Activity: The Listening Walk

1. **Warm Up:** Take two or three minutes in the classroom and ask students to simply stop and listen. Ask them what they hear. Buzzing of fluorescent lights? Paper rustling? Someone coughing? Feet moving? Breathing? This is excellent practice for the next step—the listening walk.

2. **Explain the Listening Walk:** Explain to students that everyone will now go on a listening walk. Everyone must walk silently, without talking. The only task is to listen— to listen to every sound including the ones they might be making themselves (heartbeat, jacket rubbing against a pant leg, footsteps, coughing, breathing, etc.). Tell students to try to remember as many sounds as they can.

3. **On the Walk:** Once on the walk, tell students they must try to be as quiet as possible. If going outside is not an option, a listening walk inside the school can work very well. Schools are filled with sound! The walk should last about five to ten

minutes depending on the group. If the group is capable of it, you could have them take paper and pencil, and try writing down the sounds they hear. You might want to give very young children a bag to take with them and have them pretend to put the sounds in the bag. Upon their return, have students take the imaginary sounds out of their bag and describe them.

4. **Back in the Classroom:** Once back in the classroom, have the students either discuss as a group or write down the sounds they heard. Ask them a few questions:

    —What sound was above you? Next to you? Below you?

    —What was the loudest sound? A moving sound? A remarkable sound? A sound that changed direction?

    —What sound would you like to eliminate?

    —What was your favorite sound?

    —What was the most beautiful sound?

    Expand and adapt the list of questions to your particular group of students. The important thing is to focus on listening. Ask students to notice how different the responses may be—everyone went on the same walk, but not everyone heard the same things.

5. **Assessment:** Observe students' participation in the walk and also in the follow-up discussion or writing assignment. Did they actively participate? Were they able to describe the sounds they heard? Were they also listening to the responses of others and the group discussion?

Listening Walk: Curriculum Connections

*   **Language Arts:** Speaking and listening are two key points of the English Language Arts Common Core State Standards and the TESOL Standards. Through the listening walk, students improve on complex listening skills, not only by doing

the exercise of a listening walk, but also by listening to each other's responses. Collecting the sound evidence and writing it down enhances basic writing skills and builds vocabulary. Most often students describe an object by what it looks like, not what it sounds like. The practice of listening and then finding words to describe sound demonstrates, through writing, their listening experience. To extend the lesson, have students write a narrative piece from the compiled list describing sounds in the environment, take an imaginary listening walk related to a piece of literature, or discuss the meaning of *onomatopoeia* and ask students to create words imitating sounds they heard on the listening walk.

- **Social Studies:** The listening walk can be adapted and expanded to deepen the understanding of a social studies topic. After completing the listening walk and discussing the sounds students discovered, have them make a list of what they would hear if they were someone in another time and place: a family member in a covered wagon during the Westward Movement, a revolutionary soldier in battle, an American Indian or Pilgrim at Thanksgiving, etc.

- **Mathematics:** After returning from the listening walk, ask students to list sounds that have a particular pattern, such as high-low-high-low or loud-soft-soft-loud-soft-soft. Have students create symbolic representations of the different sounds and then draw the patterns. Or, as a group, classify or categorize sounds by sound type—high, low, soft, loud, natural, metallic, etc. Do some sounds fall into more than one classification? Have students graph the different types of sounds.

- **Science:** Have students categorize the sounds by how they are generated: natural sounds, man-made sounds, human sounds. Which were most dominant? Older students could discuss the issue of noise pollution. Relate science vocabulary to sound. For example, have students make a list of *extinct* sounds. What makes a sound extinct? What are sounds that are *endangered*? Help students practice tonal discrimination. Ask them to categorize the sounds they heard by tone—high, low, medium. Discuss the concept of *frequency*. As a demonstration, fill water glasses with various amounts of water and ask students to predict whether each glass will make a higher or lower sound when tapped. Or, pull a piece of fishing line or wire tight across a big tin can or an open cardboard box. Pluck the string and listen to the sound. Make another "instrument" with a shorter piece of wire. Ask students to predict if the sound will be higher or lower.

- **Visual Arts:** After returning from the listening walk, have students choose one location they visited and instruct them to draw the sounds they heard there. Encourage students to draw the sound, not the real image. For example, if they heard wind, they should draw an abstract expression of what the wind in the tree sounded like instead of simply drawing a tree. What shape is the sound? What color or colors? Is it represented with curvy or straight lines? Have students compare their visual representations. The artist Paul Klee described melody as "taking a tone for a walk." Ask students if there was a sound they heard on the walk that was melodic. Can they sing it? What does it look like? Have students create a visual representation of a melody using line, shape, and color.

Music Across the Curriculum

Here are some simple sound and music activities that can be used at any grade level. These activities do not require any specialized musical knowledge or talent and are easy to implement with minimal preparation.

Sound Diaries

This is an excellent follow-up to the listening walk exercise. Have students take a few minutes every day to listen to sounds in a particular place. With each listening, students should describe what they hear in a sound diary. They can then draw the sounds. What do they look like visually? What color are they? What shape? This exercise can link directly to a visual arts curriculum on line, shape, and color.

Use sound diaries as a tool for expanding vocabulary. Have students write a narrative piece about the sounds they hear, describing more extensively the sounds they notice, what they wonder about, and what listening makes them think about. Adjectives most commonly used by students describe things visually, not through sound. Listening exercises bring an awareness of sound words, which can expand and enhance students' writing and link directly to language arts curriculum.

Soundscapes

Bring a story, an historical event, or a particular habitat alive with sound! Have students analyze a particular event or situation purely through sound, and then recreate it. Tell students to carefully select just the essential sounds and place them sequentially in such a way that produces an accurate reproduction of the sound environment. Students can recreate sounds with their voices, bodies, and everyday objects. Many recorded sounds are available on the Internet. Tell the audience to listen to the performance with eyes closed while the performers bring the environment immediately and accurately alive through sound alone. The audience will feel as if they are immersed in the soundscape, whether it is the rainforest, a desert oasis, a moment in the Civil War, Napoleon's March, or a moment in time from a chapter book the class is reading. The creation of soundscapes requires students to create and organize sound symbols, connecting writing, math, and storytelling skills.

Name Rhythms

Begin by having each student clap the syllables of their first and last name, creating a name rhythm. For example, this name has four syllables: Clay/ton/Tal/bert. Have the class echo the "name rhythm."

After hearing and echoing everyone's name, go around the circle again, this time just listening to each name rhythm without echoing. Tell students to listen carefully. Are there name rhythms that have the same rhythmic pattern? For example, Susan Fisher has the same name rhythm as Clayton Talbert.

The name rhythms can then be played on a rhythm instrument. If you don't have any instruments, found sounds, such as tapping a pencil on a notebook or shaking a plastic bottle with paper clips in it, work just as well. Have each person play his or her name rhythm on an instrument. Ask students to describe how these sounds are different than the clapping they did earlier.

Next, have students create a class composition, adding one name rhythm pattern on top of another. The goal of putting all the rhythms together is to create one ensemble, with all the name rhythms interacting. The idea is not to "show off" one name rhythm, but rather to create a group composition where all the name rhythms work together to form a rhythmic piece. Listen to what transpires once all the rhythms are played together. If at first the ensemble falls apart and does not seem to be in sync, that's fine. Stop and analyze how to improve it. The conversation is as important as the exercise itself. What would help to make it better? It might mean that some name rhythms, for the sake of the group ensemble, may need to be slightly adjusted: Clay/ton/Tal/bert may need to become Clay/ton/ /Tal/bert, leaving a longer space between the first two syllables and the last two syllables.

Have students record their name rhythm patterns using symbols. Ask students to draw what they think their name rhythms look like. Figure 2.1 shows an example of name rhythm symbols.

Figure 2.1 Name Rhythm Symbols

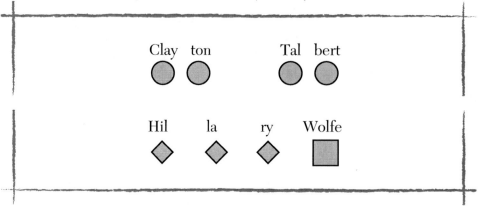

Have students compare and contrast the representations of their name rhythms. Is there someone else in the class who has his or her same name rhythm? Do they look the same? Are there some that are similar but not exactly the same? What's different? Have students play each other's name rhythms, using their drawings as a sound score.

This exercise addresses several important learning standards: recognizing patterns, transferring symbol to sound (a basic literacy skill), developing abstract reasoning skills, developing listening skills, and creating a cooperative group environment.

Sound Scores

To most of us, a familiar musical score is comprised of notes placed on a staff. This notation is commonly used around the world; however, there are multitudes of ways to notate music. Allowing students to create their own musical score, using their own symbols and scoring technique, deepens creative and critical thinking skills and abstract reasoning. A sound score is simply a map that uses symbols to indicate to the reader or "musician" how to play the composition. A sound score can also be created to document sounds. For instance, a rainstorm can be graphically notated with symbols indicating the different sounds (hands rubbing together, clapping, finger snapping, etc.). Figure 2.2 shows an example of a storm sound score.

Figure 2.2 Storm Sound Score

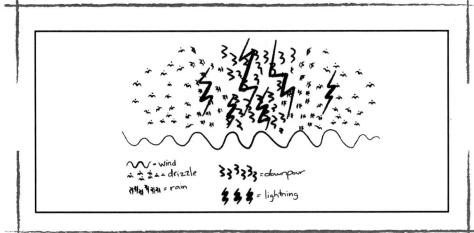

- wind
∴ ∴ ∴ ∴ = drizzle
ᵗʰⁱⁿ = rain
ᏃᏃᏃᏃᏃ = downpour
ϟ ϟ ϟ = lightning

Have students create sound scores, alone or in groups. The compositions could connect to any curriculum content—social studies, science, math, or language arts. For example, students could create sound scores representing a tornado, a scene from the Revolutionary War, the plot of a novel, or a tessellation.

Sound Exploration

Ask students to bring in interesting sounds from home. Tell them they are not looking for an instrument, but rather an everyday object that they can use to make an interesting sound. If it is difficult for students to bring in something from home, they can also use classroom objects (rulers, pencils, trash cans, erasers, notebooks, etc.) to make interesting sounds. Have students demonstrate their sounds and explain why they chose them. Tell students to describe their sounds, using sound words such as *loud, soft, metallic, percussive, natural, electronic,* etc.

Ask each student to discover three different ways to play their found object so it makes three different sounds. For instance, a student could scrape a pencil on a cheese grater, or tap the pencil on the outside of the grater, making a different kind of sound, or put the pencil inside the cheese grater and move it around.

Use students' found sounds to enhance content area learning. Have students use their mathematical skills to categorize the sounds. Ask them to notice if some sounds fall into more than one category. Have students organize the sounds in groups, choose rhythm patterns, and create a whole-class or small group composition, then represent the sounds in a graph or chart.

Have students create sound stories using the found sounds. This exercise can be done in a large group or in smaller groups. First, have students determine what else those sounds remind them of. Then, have everyone close their eyes while one student plays his or her sound in some particular way, such as scraping a pencil across a cheese grater. Ask students to think of what else it sounds like—maybe a motor starting up, or maybe a pig grunting! Perhaps running a pen down the spiral binding of a notebook may sound like a little bug. Hitting the palm of a hand on a notebook could sound like someone walking. Using these interpretations of found sounds as inspiration, have students create a story in which the sounds are used as sound effects. This exercise reinforces abstract thinking, helps students visualize the story, and builds creativity and imagination.

Songwriting

The availability of easily obtainable educational materials on the Internet provides more than enough songs to supplement any and every curriculum subject. Although these songs are often clever and can definitely support student learning, to make learning truly relevant and meaningful it is important to let students play a role in the creative aspect of songwriting. Creating and singing a song reinforces learning. We know this inherently because many adults still sing the ABC song or recite, "Thirty days hath September" without hesitation. In *Critical Links: Learning in the Arts and Student Academic and Social Development*, editor Richard Deasy (2002) cites several research studies documenting how music making increases spatial reasoning and spatial temporal reasoning, motivates writing and language arts skills, and improves language for learners of English.

When students write a song they have ownership of it, and they are much more apt to remember it. It is perfectly acceptable to use standard familiar melodies if devising a song from scratch seems like a daunting task. Having students assist in the songwriting process is ultimately more satisfying and, beyond reinforcing their learning, it enhances their creativity, imagination, and cooperative skills. As always, the process itself is a valuable endeavor. Having students create their own songs about their learning reinforces language arts skills, as well as the content area the song focuses on.

Victor Cockburn, folk musician and songwriter, provides an example of using songwriting to promote deeper understanding of a curriculum theme by creating what he calls a "pocket song"—a song short enough to fit in your pocket. This song was written with a first grade class in a ballad form (ABCB) to tell the story of the metamorphosis of tadpoles to frogs:

Tadpoles to Frogs

First the baby frogs were little eggs,
Living in the water under a lily pad.
The little eggs hatch in the spring,
The baby tadpoles are feeling glad.
They look like fish with little tails,
They are all green so they can hide away.
Then one day they start to grow little legs,
So they can jump, run, and play.

—McAvinnue School, Lowell, MA

Pocket songs get students writing about curriculum topics with just a few lines of lyrics. Singing and writing on different topics helps students explore language, practice rhyme, and expand vocabulary while eliciting lyrics and putting them to familiar melodies. As students learn more about a subject, encourage them to continue adding verses to their pocket songs.

Try having students write piggyback songs by writing new lyrics to a familiar melody. Another possibility for easy songwriting is to "zip" new verses into old songs (called *zipper songs*) such as adding a verse to "This Little Light of Mine" or adding another animal to "Old MacDonald Had a Farm."

Chants

In addition to creating songs about a particular subject matter, have students create a chant. It is the most effective way of remembering something. Chants can be made up about particular topics—the water cycle, names of the continents, long and short vowels, rules of long division, etc., or they can be about classroom rules. All that is needed is rhythm and, if desired, rhyme. Since rap is curently a well-known genre, many students are quite comfortable creating chants.

Making Instruments

There are many simple instruments that can be made with found materials. (Refer to Appendix D: Recommended Resources for books on instrument making.) Students have great fun making their own instruments, either string or percussion. This exercise can relate to science, math, and language arts. The properties of sound, sound waves, and vibration are all addressed in instrument making, which includes both science and mathematics curricula as well as patterning, listening, and analyzing sound properties. Descriptive words that describe the sound of the instrument can lead to poems, narratives, or stories, thus integrating music into language arts. Exploring onomatopoeia is another natural outcome of instrument making as well as exploring metaphor and simile. Play a rainstick. Have everyone listen. Ask students to write a poem describing the sound. What does the rain stick sound like to them? Does it remind them of something, such as a rainstorm or an ocean? Or is it a whoosh of sounds—tap, tap, tap, swish, swish, swish? Encourage students to explore the possibilities.

Sound Effect Stories

When reading books aloud to students, add sounds to enhance the story. Sounds can be verbal or created using found objects in the classroom. For example, when the billy goats are trip-trapping over the bridge, use your feet or hands to make stomping or tapping noises. If a doorbell rings, sing out "ding-dong." On subsequent readings, have students provide the soundtrack. Students can also create songs and chants based on the story or using the actual words from the book. Add sound effects to nonfiction content area reading as well. If the class is reading about frogs, have students make frog noises. When reading about tornadoes, a large whooshing noise is appropriate. Be sure to have a nonverbal "stop" signal in place to bring a quick end to the sounds.

Singing Games

There are many playground chants, clapping games, and traditional singing games that are part of every culture. As part of a social studies unit, bring in traditional games and songs to enhance the understanding of the culture or time period being studied. For instance, in Ghana, stone passing games are played by children on the playground. Jump rope rhymes are part of many cultures. Figure 2.3 shows some great resources for games and songs from around the world. See Appendix D: Recommended Resources for more information.

Figure 2.3 Singing Games Resources

World Music Press (Danbury, Connecticut) publishes a collection of songs and games, many with CDs, from Africa, the Caribbean, Europe, Latin America, and multiple cultures.

West Music carries many world music songbooks and collections.

Some recommended recordings include:

- *Step It Down, Step It Down: Games, Plays, Songs, and Stories from the Afro-American Heritage* by Bessie Jones

- Putumayo's *World Playground* CDs

- *Qu Qu Qu Barg-e-Chinaar: Children's Songs from Afghanistan*

Traditional Folk Songs

Folk songs provide a rich resource for understanding culture, tradition, and history to enhance social studies curriculum. There are many available resources that provide songs from many cultures as well as songs from American history, such as the Civil War, Revolutionary War, songs about building the railroad, songs written by women in the mills…the list is endless. The book *The Folk Songs of North America*, by Alan Lomax (1975) is a valuable resource and contains music and origins of over 300 songs, from ballads to spirituals, from every region of the United States. There are also informative videos available that give students authentic insight into a particular period of history through the Smithsonian Folkways videos, available on the Smithsonian website. Begin by having students read the lyrics, analyzing what the songwriter is trying to convey about his or her condition. Quite often, as in the case of the Revolutionary War, students can compare two songs, expressing two different points of view.

Assessment

Classroom assessment for any integrated music lesson must take into consideration curriculum goals and music goals as well as the diversity of learners. Using the process of backward design, ask yourself, what do I want my students to learn in music? What do I want them to learn in the content areas? How can I best assess a student's work in both music and the content areas?

First, identify music learning goals. For example, goals for the listening walk activity could include that students participate fully in the walk, listen carefully, and describe the sounds they hear. There is not one correct set of "answers" in the listening walk activity that can be assessed by a test, but rather the goal is for students to deepen their awareness of the sounds in the environment and be able to describe them in a variety of ways. A checklist or rubric could be used to assess the quality of listening that occurred, along with assessment of their written sound descriptions. In an activity where students create and perform music, assessment might include observation of student performances using a rubric. Audio or video recording can be very helpful in this kind of assessment.

To assess content area learning, evidence should be collected to show how students demonstrate their understanding of the content through music and sound. For example, if students are asked to write a narrative based on their listening walk experience, the work could be assessed using a narrative writing rubric. If the content area being addressed is patterning in mathematics, the patterns students create should be assessed as well as students' explanations of their work. If the content area is social studies and students are asked to create a soundscape of a revolutionary battlefield, assessment should include whether the sounds students describe are appropriate for that environment. The rubric in Figure 2.4 could be used to assess a soundscape activity in language arts.

Figure 2.4 Assessment Rubric for Soundscape in Language Arts

Assignment: Create a soundscape that invokes the themes and concepts of a novel using both found sounds and originally created sounds.

Assessment Criteria	Advanced	Proficient	Developing
Demonstrates understanding of themes and concepts in the novel	Soundscape demonstrates deep understanding of concepts and themes	Soundscape demonstrates understanding of concepts and themes	Soundscape does not demonstrate understanding of concepts and themes
Selects found sounds and creates original sounds	Selects interesting and unexpected sounds and creatively produces original sounds	Selects appropriate sounds and creates some original sounds	Selects inappropriate sounds and/or does not create original sounds
Layers and sequences sounds to create an aural environment	Layers and sequences sounds creatively; creates mood and brings listener into environment	Layers and sequences sound appropriately; creates mood	Does not layer sounds; sequences inappropriately

Concluding Thoughts

Music-making creates a more humanistic, caring community that encourages recognizing, listening to, and celebrating every voice. Our schools, now more diverse than ever before, must have spaces made for individual and community voices to be recognized and honored. Nick Page (1995) claims that making music together helps to "democratize" the community, giving everyone an opportunity to become the leader and feel ownership. Once this mindset is embraced, enormous possibilities open up, not only for music, but also for all the arts: dance, poetry, visual arts, drama. There is much to gain once we rid ourselves of the limiting categories such as singer/non-singer, dancer/non-dancer, artist/non-artist, etc. When cultural and societal boundaries are broken down, minds are released and creativity enlisted (Pascale 2006).

Music making, in all its iterations, brings people together, builds community, and creates a sense of belonging and common purpose, both to celebrate the diversity of music expression that characterizes the human condition, and to suggest that music making is open to all. The focus should not be on a hierarchy of talent, where one singer is superior to another, but rather the communal voice (Page 1995). Equally important, it strengthens learning and provides for assessment of students in innovative ways that recognize learning differences. Integrating music teaches students, at the most basic level, to listen, to correct, and to pursue excellence (Page 1995). Including musical activities as part of the teaching and learning palette strengthens student learning. It is most certainly not about whether we sing beautifully or in tune or read notes perfectly from a musical score. It is about creating a learning environment that stimulates and engages students with excitement, connection, and relevance.

As educators, we are faced daily with the stimulating challenge of teaching students who all have a great potential to learn. Our task is to investigate each student's abilities through multiple lenses so that each reaches their full potential. Integrating music into the curriculum offers a powerful option for learning.

Reflection

1. What is your musical culture? What songs did you grow up singing or what music did you or your family listen to? What would play on your personal musical jukebox?

2. How varied is the musical culture of your students? How can you honor those differences?

3. What do you notice when your class participates in a musical activity, like singing or making up a chant? What changes in the room? Do you see a change in students who are often not engaged?

4. Choose one content area lesson you intend to teach in the next month. How could you integrate music in teaching the content?

Chapter 3

Anchoring Curriculum in Storytelling

A good story transports you to another world, introduces you to fascinating characters and invites you into their lives. Whether it's from a page, on a screen, or from personal experience, a good story has the power to change people.

Storytelling in its most basic form is an art that has been around since the beginning of time. "Cultures from around the world have used storytelling as a way to preserve memories, share values and beliefs, instruct, and entertain. Long before written records, storytellers taught through an oral tradition" (Norfolk 2010).

Stories, whether fables, fairytales, or stories from one's own life, are one of the most basic ways of sharing knowledge, of making sense of experiences, and of seeing oneself in relation to others. "In the classroom, storytelling is an important activity because it has strong links to literacy. In our fast-paced, media-driven world, storytelling can be a nurturing way to remind children that spoken words are powerful, that listening is important, and that clear communication between people is an art" (Story Arts 2000).

What Is Storytelling?

Storytelling is the act of using language and gesture in colorful ways to create scenes in a sequence. A storyteller's cultural background and uniqueness shines through in the choice of words and gestures she/he chooses. Story time, in any form, is magical.

—Gere, Kozlovich, and Kelin (2002)

Stories exercise the imagination and build literacy skills. Language is shared, representing objects and ideas. By simply sharing a story from a summer vacation or what happened during the day, the storyteller is able to play with words and the subtleties of inflection and gesture. The uniqueness and true identity of the storyteller is shared with the listeners.

Storytelling, often thought of as an art form to be used only with young children, is a powerful learning tool for all ages, and when effectively implemented can be successful with elementary through college level students. For most of us, reading stories to children is a natural teaching technique. As teachers, we understand the power of hearing stories and reading stories to children. There's a magic that happens when you are swept away with the written word. A good story transports you into another world, introducing you to interesting characters and sharing insights into their lives. Stories can make you laugh and cry, and have the power to change your feelings and perspectives.

Both are valuable teaching tools, but there is significant difference between reading stories and telling stories. Both formats strengthen literacy skills and directly connect to English language and Common Core State Standards. Language development through narrative, knowledge of language structure, reflection, creativity, critical thinking, and spoken, written, and visual language are all enhanced through reading or telling a story.

What Is the Difference Between Reading a Story and Telling a Story?

When a story is read aloud from a book, the audience and the reader are focused on the book. The reader is reading the text, and the audience is looking at the pictures. The reader may read in the voices of the characters or add sound effects, but neither the reader nor the listeners have an effect on the story itself.

Storytelling is powerful in ways that go beyond reading a story, and it benefits both the listener and the storyteller. One of the powerful aspects of storytelling is that it is co-creative and interactive. The storyteller, using narrative structure and mental imagery, communicates with an audience who are also using mental imagery, and together they create the story. A storyteller, through the use of language and gestures, is able to create scenes in the mind of the listener. It is the listener who, through imagination and visualization, is able to enhance the story and bring it to life. Reading a story aloud can accomplish this to some extent, however, the power of the storyteller to bring the story to life, through not only voice, but also body and emotion, makes the experience more personal. Just as hearing a live musical performance is an intense personal experience for the listener, listening to a story told by a storyteller provides an experience that becomes in itself more personal and intimate.

A story read from a book does not change, but a storyteller constantly gauges the listeners' reactions to the performance, adjusting as the story goes on. For example, if a particular line or movement makes the audience laugh, the storyteller might repeat it, or emphasize a similar line or gesture throughout the story. If the listeners are showing signs of losing interest, the storyteller might raise the energy level and make broader gestures, which in turn changes the listeners' focus. The storyteller can ask the listeners to participate by repeating lines or offer the listeners choices as to where the story should go. There is an interplay between the storyteller and the listeners that influences the story itself.

Why Does Storytelling Matter?

Storytelling is a powerful teaching and learning tool. "Imagination and visualization are essential literacy skills and are the very tools that allow a reader to give meaning to the words being decoded which in turn lead to comprehension and retention" (Norfolk 2010). When a student is asked to not only listen to a story but also summarize it and repeat it back or retell it, learning increases. Visualization and imagination come into play and memory is enhanced. Often teachers remark that once they begin using storytelling techniques in the classroom, students' engagement in active listening is magnified. In addition, many teachers share that, much to their surprise, their most reluctant readers are eager to participate and share in the discussions about the story.

Storytelling benefits not only the listeners, but the storyteller as well. The act of storytelling encourages active listening, builds analytical skills, and increases retention and comprehension. Literacy skills are greatly enhanced. "Oral narratives are an important link to literacy. Narratives serve as a transition with familiar and past topics and often assist children in moving from the sharing function of conversations to the teaching function of written language by imparting lessons based on one's experiences. Oral narratives have been linked to school success reflected in emergent literacy. Labeling to listing to connecting to sequencing to narrating all occur, over time, in the process of storytelling" (McCabe and Rolins 1994). You cannot tell a story without being engaged physically, mentally, and emotionally. Organization, sequencing skills, and creative thinking are all required. A child uses event knowledge to carry on discourse for multiple purposes: to frame language structures, to learn and use new words, to engage in fantasy play, to make up stories, to remember specific happenings, and to form object categorization (Carr 2001).

Both familiar and new language patterns are heard and learned through storytelling. The act of thinking and reflecting occurs through storytelling. Both tellers and listeners have the opportunity to relate the story to their own lives and reflect and make connections. Storytelling, like other art forms, allows children who do not feel competent reading or writing to excel through an art form that uses a combination of other language and expressive arts. A story is a powerful vehicle for sharing multiple perspectives and transmitting cultural values.

When creating a story, students use a wide range of communication strategies. In the process of creating a story, they are applying knowledge of language structure and language conventions, conducting research, participating in reflective, creative, and critical thinking, and using spoken, written, and visual language. They are using a combination of skills and processes to create narrative linked to real or imagined events in a clear sequence.

Storytelling has a positive effect on the classroom community. When a story is told or retold, there is an immediate connection that is made between the storyteller and the audience. The audience becomes engaged in a shared experience that is quite different from hearing a story read aloud. Recent research has shown that "when one person tells a story and the other actively listens, their brains actually begin to synchronize" (Dooley 2010).

Everyone has a story to tell, and sharing stories provides an effective vehicle for giving voice to the teacher and the students. The act of sharing stories builds community, strengthens appreciation for one another, and allows many perspectives to be heard and considered. When students tell their stories, it is their moment to have their voice honored. Stories provide a powerful vehicle for addressing issues such as bullying, racism, and bias around ability, gender, race, and sexual orientation. By hearing the voices of others, students build cultural bridges and have the opportunity to share their own personal stories. This can be powerful and insightful. Many points of view can be heard in a safe and respectful environment when students are able to tell their own and listen to others' personal stories.

The importance of building a strong and trusting classroom community cannot be underestimated. Through storytelling, a solid team environment is established and the possibilities for successful teaching and learning increase dramatically. Interestingly, this is similar to the phenomenon of "entrainment" in music making. Entrainment, quite simply, is one pulse imitating another pulse. Teachers are often aware that the speed of their speech and actions affects their students. Our rhythms and speech copy each other (Page 1995). When people are engaged in any of the performing arts such as storytelling, drama, music, or dance, there is potential to have a mutual influence on one another both emotionally and physically.

Common Core

Storytelling in the Common Core State Standards

The Common Core State Standards outline the expectation of young children to use a combination of drawing, dictating, and writing to narrate a single event where they recount two or more sequenced events including some detail. Older children are expected to write and recount in narrative well-elaborated events including details that describe action, thoughts, and feelings. All of these standards are met through engagement in storytelling.

When digital storytelling is implemented, a variety of technological and information resources are used to create and gather information, addressing the Common Core State Standards through using technology to produce and publish writing.

How to Become a Storyteller

Storytelling is a skill that can be easily learned and it involves techniques that can be integrated into any subject or lesson. Storyteller Meg Lippert explains, "Teachers are often intimidated by the idea that they have to 'memorize' a story to tell it. Nothing is further from the truth. In fact, it is often possible to tell a short folk tale having heard the story once, if the listener is picturing the story unfold in sequence. Then all the teacher has to do is retell the story as they 'watch' it unfold" (Lippert, pers. comm.). Once we as teachers work through our own fears and develop confidence and storytelling repertoire, it becomes much easier to share stories with students. Stories naturally build community. The outcome of sharing stories with students is that students are much more eager to continue to learn and tell new stories to practice their oral fluency, the bridge to effective reading and writing.

Start with Personal Stories and Folk Tales

Anyone can become a good storyteller because we all have stories to tell. One of the best ways to begin is with a story that is very familiar, such as a family or personal story. Personal stories are a good place to start because they quite naturally come from an oral tradition and have never been written down. Most importantly, there is no one "right" way to tell a personal story. Tell about the time your brother dressed up as a ghost and scared you, or how Aunt Mika made a spice cake with whole cloves instead of ground cloves and everyone got quite a bit of spice when they took the first bite!

If students have trouble thinking of a personal story, try asking questions, such as:

- Have you ever laughed so hard you fell out of your chair?

- How did you learn to swim or ride a bike?

- Have you ever been really scared?

- Have you ever done something you are proud of?

- Do you have stories about your family, friends, or neighbors?

- What is your favorite thing to do? Why?

If no events come to mind, having them listen to other stories will help stir up memories.

An easy next step is to focus on folk tales, which are also from the oral tradition. Once you have learned the sequence of events, you can tell a story in your own words. There are many, many folk tale collections and folk tale picture books that provide excellent resources (see the list in Figure 3.1). Explore your school and/or public library (folk tales are in section 398.2) and hunt for books that are written by storytellers. Any folk tales published by storytellers Martha Hamilton and Mitch Weiss, Margaret Read MacDonald, Won-Ldy Paye and Meg H. Lippert, Anne Pellowski, or Diane Wolkstein will be written in language that flows naturally in oral speech patterns. In addition, these sources will include background information about the cultures from which the stories come. There are many newly published folk tales and audio recordings of stories now available in bookstores. Listening to recordings of stories helps provide a feel for oral cadences and vocal possibilities.

A List Of Stories to Get You Started

To get started, try one of the stories found in Figure 3.1. Some of these you probably already know! Any of these are excellent choices for beginning student storytellers. When you and your students become familiar with the patterns of these tales, you can easily use them to create your own stories.

Figure 3.1 Stories to Start With

Stories in which one thing leads to the next:

"The Tailor" in Nancy Schimmel's *Just Enough to Make a Story*

Head, Body, Legs: A Story from Liberia by Won-Ldy Paye and Meg Lippert (picture book)

"What a Wonderful Life" in Margaret Read MacDonald's *Shake-it-Up Tales!*

Stories in which one misunderstanding leads to another:

"Lazy Jack" in Joseph Jacobs's *English Fairy Tales*

"Hic Hic Hic" in Margaret Read MacDonald's *Twenty Tellable Tales*

"Soap, Soap, Soap" in Richard Chase's *Grandfather Tales*

Stories in which a character consults a series of other characters to solve a problem:

The Squeaky Door by Margaret Read MacDonald (picture book)

"The Wide Mouth Frog" in Margaret Read MacDonald's *Parent's Guide to Storytelling*

Stories in which things get larger and larger, then end with something small:

"The Lost Mitten" in Margaret Read MacDonald's *Parent's Guide to Storytelling*

The Turnip by Pierr Morgan (picture book)

The Gingerbread Boy by Pail Galdone (picture book)

Stories to tell with paper:

"Brothers Tall and Brothers Small" in Anne Pellowski's *The Family Storytelling Handbook*

"The Rain Hat" in Nancy Schimmel's *Just Enough to Make a Story*

Drawing stories:

"The Black Cat" in Anne Pellowski's *The Story Vine*

"The King's Diamond Cross" in Anne Pellowski's *The Storytelling Handbook*

Audience participation/action:

"Jack and the Robbers" in Margaret Read MacDonald's *Twenty Tellable Tales*

"Little Boy Frog and Little Boy Snake" in Margaret Read MacDonald's *Shake-It-Up Tales!*

(McPhie, MacDonald, and Lippert workshop handout 2011).

Note: Full bibliographic entries for these resources can be found in Appendix D, Recommended Resources.

Make the Story Your Own

It is very important for a storyteller to make a story his or her own. If there is a story that you like but find it doesn't quite meet your needs, try to seek out several versions and then create your own, using some of the strategies described by storyteller and former elementary school teacher Meg Lippert (2005):

- Identify the qualities of the characters and infuse your telling with these. Add dialogue, gestures, or movement to convey a sense of wiliness, sloth, or wisdom. If there are animal characters in the story, play with animal sounds and character voices.

- Many stories benefit from humor in word play, characterizations, or unexpected events. If there are places you can insert humorous elements, try them. They may become treasured moments.

- Remember the setting. This element is often missing from folk tales in collections, yet it is important to share clues that will let your listeners know where and when the story takes place. Just mentioning a palm tree or a blackberry bush may help them relax into the surroundings and join you in the imagined story place.

- Amid all your tinkering with the story, remember the underlying message. Is it about overcoming pain, dealing with adversity, sustaining hope, or caring for others? After adjusting the story for the elements listed above, ask yourself, "Did I retain the heart of the story?"

Getting Students to Tell Their Own Stories

Leader Kevin Cordi of Voices of Illusion: Youth Storytelling in California strongly believes that the most important aspect of storytelling is for students to experience telling stories to each other. "The most important audience for students is themselves. I have watched how quickly a sense of group cohesion builds from not only youth telling stories, but youth listening to stories and from this exchange other youth build ideas for stories and begin loving them. In this environment, a sense of community grows; a community that cares about each other and a community that shares with one another. There is a positive sense of value for the growth of not only a person's story but the person himself" (Norfolk 2010, 149).

Introductory Activity: Step-By-Step Process for Learning to Tell a Story

Below is storyteller Meg Lippert's easy-to-follow, step-by-step process to guide students to successfully telling their own stories (used with permission). The story can be related to any content area: a folktale or fable, a historical event, a scientific process or concept (e.g., how a caterpillar becomes a butterfly, the water cycle), or a series of math problems (e.g., ten cookies disappear in groups until they are all gone, cells multiply by splitting repeatedly).

1. **Tell:** Tell a simple story to students, using voice and gesture to help the story come to life.

2. **Retell:** Help students retell the story as a group, with volunteers adding parts in sequence. If students start retelling a story from a point in the middle of the story, respond, "Yes, that is correct, and what happened before that?" Encourage students to add voice and gesture to make the story more engaging.

3. **Review:** Review the story structure, listing the major elements of the story on the board. Go over the beginning, ending, and any key dialog. When students know how the story starts and how it ends, the story will flow more fluently. Remind students to visualize the story, and to describe what they "see" rather than focusing on the exact words of the story.

4. **Tell to the Wall:** Ask each student to find a place in the classroom facing a wall. Tell students that when you give them a signal, they are to begin telling the story, as if they were telling it to someone else. When they finish, discuss the experience with the class. Did they get stuck? Which parts flowed smoothly? (Hamilton and Weiss 2005, 103)

5. **Tell to a Partner:** Pair students with partners and ask them to tell the stories to one another. If time is short, ask them to take turns, with one starting the story and telling half way through and their partner telling the rest of the story.

6. **Celebrate!** Within 30 minutes your students are storytellers. Encourage them to tell the story to their family and friends. Provide opportunities for them to tell the story to another class at their grade level or to younger children in their school. Remind them that when their families ask them, "What did you learn in school today?" they have a new story to tell. Have students keep a list of tales they know so they can begin to build a repertoire they can retell to share their learning, and entertain themselves, their friends, and their families.

From Telling to Writing: Getting Students to Write Their Stories

It's a small step from getting students telling their stories to getting students writing their stories. To begin, make certain students have heard and can tell several stories with a traditional structure. With students, choose a familiar story and break it into components to identify the character qualities, the plot sequence, and the ending using the *Making a Story* structure (Figure 3.2). When students understand this story structure, have them write their own stories based on a character they create themselves, following the structure. This can be a pre-writing activity that leads to students writing more complete and more clearly structured stories (Meg Lippert, pers. comm.).

Figure 3.2 *Making a Story* Structure

Making a Story

1. **Who** is your story about?

    What kind of character/animal is your character?

    How big or small is your character?

    What does your character look like?

    What is your character wearing?

    What does your character like?

    What does your character want or need?

    What is your character afraid of?

    What is your character's name?

2.   **How** does the character get what he or she wants or needs?

    Try out different scenarios and see what is the most interesting and imaginative.

3. **What** is the title of the story? Make a list of several ideas and then choose one.

Storytelling Across the Curriculum

Once your students are familiar and comfortable with storytelling, try some of these simple storytelling ideas that can be used at any grade level.

Storytelling in Social Studies

Tell historical stories to bring history to life for students. Meg Lippert says, "When studying New York colonial history and Westward Expansion, I taught all the content and concepts through a narrative focused on one young girl, Ann Lawrence of Old New York, based on the historical fiction book of that title by Gladys Malvern, learning a chapter a day and telling it to the students. Then I simply moved Ann and her family westward, on a flatboat down the Mississippi, as the year progressed" (Lippert, pers. comm.). The students, once they are familiar with the content, can then add to the story, building on the basic framework. Storyteller Kathy Currie tells the story of Esther Samuel, a woman who traveled the Oregon Trail from Independence, Missouri to The Dalles, Oregon. Once students hear these types of stories, they can, through research and reading, build their own repertoire of stories from a particular time period or moment in history.

Storytelling in Science

Storytelling can help students grasp complicated scientific concepts and processes by requiring them to break the content down and then reassemble it in sequence. Here are some stories and experiments that work well together (Sima 2012).

- **Scientific Method:** Explore the elements of the scientific method through a story, expanding on the processes of observation, problem statement, and idea generation. Experiments and experimental design can be explored through a story about a scientist who carries out a skillfully planned, carefully organized, and cleverly conducted experiment.

- **Spiders:** Tell a spider story, such as "Anansi and the Moss Covered Rock" or "Why the Spider Has a Small Waist," and then have students research or read how spiders build webs and find food and tell what they have learned via stories.

- **Metamorphosis, Frogs:** Tell a frog story, such as "How the Frog Lost Its Tail," then have students learn about metamorphosis from egg to tadpole to adult frog and tell stories to show what they know.

- **Chemical Change, Fire:** Tell "The Snooks Family" or "Twist-Mouth Family," both stories of how family members have trouble blowing out candles. Experiment with baking soda and vinegar to form carbon dioxide, which will extinguish a lighted candle, and have students create stories about the process.

- **Astronomy:** Share with students several American Indian stories about why we have day and night or why we have seasons before they learn the scientific explanation. Then, have students create their own stories to explain scientific phenomena.

Storytelling in Mathematics

Sometimes students have difficulty understanding a concept in mathematics, and even using concrete examples and manipulatives does not seem to help. How can teachers supplement the use of manipulatives to help boost children's understanding in mathematics? Zemelman, Daniels, and Hyde (1998) recommend that students discuss, write, read, and listen to mathematical ideas in order to deepen their understanding of difficult concepts. Using storytelling as a catalyst to mathematics instruction is one enjoyable and versatile method to do just this because it appeals to students' imaginations and emotions and helps make learning more meaningful. When students listen to stories, they create mental images that belong to them, connecting the content to something personally significant.

In the Classroom

Using storytelling helps students deepen their concept of place value by connecting it to an experience. One example comes from Mary Barr Goral and Cindy Meyers Gnadinger, elementary math teachers, who, in the interest of helping their students understand place value, made up a story about Queen Arithma's Party—a story of a Queen who was throwing a big party and needed to organize hundreds of invitations. Even though the experience was a fantasy story, the character in the story had a real problem that needed to be solved and using place value helped solve the problem. Students had to work in groups to bundle the invitations into groups of hundreds, tens, and ones to figure out how many invitations there were. Listening to the story and participating in problem solving related to the story helped reinforce the concept and met the standard. (Goral and Gnadinger 2006)

Have students tell the story of an equation, bringing "story problems" to life. Students can also create stories based on graphs and charts. What story does the data tell? For geometry, have students create stories about various shapes meeting one another. What happens when a trapezoid meets a rectangle? What do they have in common? What conflict might they have? Telling stories is a natural way to reinforce patterning. Most stories have a sequential pattern to them. Have students identify and represent these patterns visually or mathematically.

Storytelling and Visual Arts

Have students create content-related stories and then tell them through visual representation. Or, conversely, have students create visual works about curricular content and then compose stories based on those visual representations.

Moving between different "languages" stimulates students to use analysis, synthesis, and evaluation, the highest levels of thinking.

In the Classroom

Visual arts teacher Jessica Holloway uses storytelling in her classes to create context and deeper meaning for art projects. For example, in fifth grade she tells the story *Tunjur! Tunjur! Tunjur!: A Palestinian Folktale* (MacDonald 2006) about a childless woman who prays to Allah for progeny and is rewarded with a mischievous little cooking pot with human attributes. It gives context to the ceramic face jugs that students are making. Students sketch facial expressions and create a pot expression in clay. As a culminating activity, students create tags to tell the viewer what their pot's "mouth is full of," just like the story. The story helps students imagine which materials in a mouth would result in which face.

Storytelling and Music

A ballad is a story poem with a strong rhyme and rhythm. Many of them focus on tales from history. Have students listen to a few ballads and then try creating a group ballad about their content-area learning.

Digital Storytelling

Digital storytelling combines the art of storytelling with a variety of digital multimedia such as images, audio, and video. Digital stories bring together some mixture of digital graphics, text, recorded audio narration, video, and music to present a narrative. As with traditional storytelling, digital stories revolve around a chosen theme and particular viewpoint. The stories are typically only a few minutes long and include personal tales, retellings of historical events, or information on a particular subject.

Before students are able to create their own digital stories, they need to view several examples. Once they have experienced learning new material through this multimedia venue, they are much more apt to create their own. There are several websites that inform and instruct educators on the nuances of digital storytelling (see Appendix D: Recommended Resources).

Assessment

Arts integration assessment should always include goals and objectives in both the art and content areas. Determine at the outset what the lesson or unit goals are in both of these areas, and then design assessment to measure how students have made progress toward these goals. Because storytelling is a verbal and visual art, much of the assessment will be observational. Video recording can be very helpful as it gives you more time to observe.

Create a rubric, checklist, or rating sheet of skills and fill it out as you observe the students telling their stories. Determine what content is to be learned, communicate these expectations to students, and add this information to your observational assessment tool. Be sure that students have a copy of the checklist or rubric as they are creating their stories. When the content that is being assessed is stated specifically, students can show what they have learned and you can assess whether they have achieved those goals. In addition, be sure to leave room within your assessment to record the unanticipated learning that often takes place with arts integration.

The rating sheet shown in Figure 3.3 assesses both storytelling/ language arts skills and content area skills in math.

Figure 3.3 Checklist for Assessing Mathematical Equation Storytelling

Assignment: Create and tell a story that has a mathematical equation as its main focus.

Circle Rating	Storytelling/Language Arts: Story Elements
1 2 3 4 5	Includes a clear main idea
1 2 3 4 5	Includes supporting details
1 2 3 4 5	Uses appropriate vocabulary
1 2 3 4 5	Organizes/sequences ideas
	Speaking Skills
1 2 3 4 5	Uses appropriate and varied voice level
1 2 3 4 5	Articulates clearly
1 2 3 4 5	Uses gesture, facial expression, and other nonverbal communication
1 2 3 4 5	Engages audience
	Mathematics
1 2 3 4 5	Demonstrates understanding of the process of building the equation
1 2 3 4 5	Includes all components of the equation
1 2 3 4 5	Demonstrates understanding of the process of solving the equation
1 2 3 4 5	Successfully solves the equation and includes the solution in the story
Notes:	

Use assessment tools, such as checklists or rubrics, not only as summative assessment to show what students have learned, but also as formative assessment to help them make their stories stronger.

Students should be assessed not only on their storytelling, but on their listening and response as well. In the area of listening, some of the skills that can be assessed include understanding spoken communication, interpretation of nonverbal communication, listening for specific information, understanding main idea and details, and asking questions to clarify understanding. A listening skills rubric or checklist can be used, as well as having students create written or visual responses to the stories they hear.

Concluding Thoughts

It is has been claimed by many that storytelling is the heart and soul of education. It allows diverse points of view to be presented, it provides a place for personal histories and prior experiences to be shared, and it allows students with a wide range of linguistic abilities and ethnic backgrounds to come together and learn.

All people have a basic need to share stories. They are a way to organize experiences and record important occurrences. And stories are of great significance in language and literacy development, especially when considering the increased linguistic and cultural diversity of classrooms today (Koki 1998).

Once a story is told orally and the details of that story are memorized and shared, capturing the story in writing becomes much easier. Listeners also benefit through encountering both familiar and new language patterns. Hearing language is the first step in recreating it, both orally and in written form.

Stories are one of the most effective ways, at any level of schooling, to pass on factual information. Historical events remain in a student's mind when communicated by narrative. The ways of other cultures, both ancient and living, acquire honor in story. The facts about how plants and animals develop, how numbers work, or how government policy influences history—any topic, for that matter—can be incorporated into story form and made more memorable if the listener takes the story to heart (Dudding 2005).

We would be unwise to not use this ancient art form in our classrooms. It is through storytelling that we are able to address connections to the diverse sociocultural landscape of society, its power in the classroom, and how to most effectively serve increasingly diverse student populations. All these and more provide evidence of the need for and the power of story.

Reflection

1. Select one planned lesson you intend to use in the next month. How can you integrate storytelling into that lesson?

2. What will the assessment for this integrated lesson look like?

3. Teach the lesson and observe students as they tell their stories. What did you notice about students' levels of motivation and engagement? Why do you think this is?

Chapter 4

The Power of Dramatic Inquiry

What Is Drama?

When you hear the word *drama*, what do you think of? Often teachers initially confuse drama with theater, envisioning a staged performance with lights, costumes, and sets. They imagine their students as actors memorizing lines. Too often, they believe that they cannot bring this work into their classroom. While dramatic work can lead to this kind of performance, process drama offers a whole different experience in educational settings. Theater is focused on developing a final product for an audience. Drama, on the other hand, is focused on the process of exploration— on the growth and imagination of its participants. It uses improvisation, or acting choices that unfold in the moment, rather than memorizing scripts. Drama is about learning rather than putting on a polished performance. Focusing on the dramatic investigation is the main goal of dramatic inquiry—investigation of ideas, stories, historical moments, scientific discoveries, etc.

By becoming characters, creating and exploring a particular context or situation, students have a sense of entering into the story itself, which creates a deeper connection to the work, and provides opportunities to explore character, context, and perspective.

Former middle school teacher Jeffrey Wilhelm defines drama strategies as exploring scenarios where students "imagine to learn" (Wilhelm and Edmiston 1998). Cecily O'Neill describes drama as "a dramatic 'elsewhere,' a fictional world, which will be inhabited for the insights, interpretations, and understandings it may yield" (1995, 12). Drama can also be thought of as the use of body, voice, and imagination to explore the stories of our world (Donovan 2005). Thinking of drama in this way provides opportunities for students to use their imaginations to enter into curriculum in new ways and to explore ideas from a range of vantage points. In drama integration, the teacher learns side by side with students as they explore new landscapes of learning.

In the Classroom

What does integrated drama look like in the classroom? Tacoma, Washington, middle school science teacher Kalee Alexander uses drama to move beyond memorization and help her students grasp difficult concepts. After her students view cells under a microscope, Kalee uses dramatic techniques to have students imagine themselves as organelles and the whole classroom as a cell. Students must consider the organelles' dynamic structure and their work within cell structures. Students construct deeper knowledge through this exploration and Kalee is better able to dispel misconceptions as students work. She notes, "It's not enough just to know the vocabulary. It's more to understand what that vocabulary means, and one way we can understand what something means is by looking at it through many different lenses. So in an attempt...to make an organelle—which is very abstract—more concrete, I thought it would be very effective to act it. And it gives [students] inspiration" (Bellisario and Donovan with Prendergast 2012).

Why Does Drama Matter?

The purpose of playing, whose end, both at first and now, was and is, to hold, as 'twere, the mirror up to nature.

—Hamlet (Shakespeare)

Research has shown that engagement in drama can deepen comprehension, bolster language skills, and develop awareness of and sensitivity to multiple perspectives (Wilhelm 2002). It can support the development of communication fluency and increase motivation for learning.

Drama, by its nature, provides the possibility to examine life's most complex issues. The process serves as a hands-on tool for exploring complex social issues, relationships, and the nature of cause and effect. It provides the opportunity to "try on" different roles and courses of action to see how role and personal choice affect circumstance in a controlled laboratory setting. The goal of the work is not to achieve one right solution, but rather to try many different potential approaches to investigate a story, issue, or moment. In this way students can fully analyze the nuances of the situation. By placing students inside a moment or event, they are able to see their role in its outcome, understand the views of others, and learn how they might have an impact. Process drama provides a window to understanding how relationships of power work and requires participants to consider vantage points different from their own.

Drama in the Common Core State Standards

Participation in drama, both as an actor and an active audience member, addresses many of the listening and speaking Common Core State Standards, such as collaboration with diverse partners, building on others' ideas, adapting speech to a variety of contexts, and evaluating a speaker's point of view. By assuming a dramatic role, students view a text from the inside out and take on many vantage points, thus analyzing the structure of texts, assessing how point of view or purpose shapes a text, making logical inferences from text, determining central ideas or themes, and analyzing how individuals, events, and ideas develop and interact over the course of a text, as stated in the Anchor Standards for Reading.

Engagement

A common complaint of students is education's lack of relevance to their lives, "Why do I have to know this?" Research shows that for students who drop out of school, the disconnect begins as early as fourth grade (Harpaz 2009). There is so much content to be learned, and so many skills to be developed, that too often the real-world connections and engagement that students need are put in the "only if we have time" category. The integration of drama in the classroom can help build the bridge between content knowledge, skills, and relevance to students' lives.

Drama can offer ways of learning that generate interest in students who have otherwise lost interest. By illuminating facets of students that teachers were unaware of, drama provides experiences in the classroom that allow each student to find his or her own voice (Gallas 1991; McCaslin 2000). Engagement in drama appeals to a variety of learning styles, allowing students to connect with the work according to how they learn. In the last few decades, much of what the arts can accomplish has been fueled by Howard Gardner's work on multiple intelligences. Gardner proposes that there are nine kinds of intelligence, or ways of learning: linguistic, logical-mathematical, spatial, kinesthetic, musical, interpersonal, intrapersonal, existentialistic, and naturalistic (Gardner 1983). Current thinking in brain research and the call for supporting variable learners support the use of multiple ways of accessing curriculum, engaging with content, and representing understanding (Center for Applied Special Technology). Most curricula focus on learning that appeals to the first two intelligences: linguistic and logical-mathematical. The arts span all of these intelligences and as a result, provide a useful method to tap into students' diverse learning styles. Gardner's work encourages an expanded view of the arts and their relationship to education (McCaslin 2000).

One of the benefits of drama in the classroom is the development of students' voices. Often, students lack confidence in expressing who they are. By exploring ideas of characters different from themselves, students locate their own ideas, values, and belief systems. They are no longer passive and accepting of the text and information that they are being presented with. Instead they learn to question, research, discover, and build their own opinions. In their investigations of a range of characters, contexts, and stories, students develop the ability to be aware of their own voice as well as the voices of others. They consider how voice works in relationship with others. And, they have the opportunity to develop and expand modes of expression and communication (Donovan 2005).

As Rachel Mattson notes, "the core of this work lies in the process of discovering ideas, not in the preparation for any kind of public presentation" (Mattson 2008, 102). Maxine Greene advocates providing students with access to the arts in order to energize them to "wide-awakeness." Engaging with art can lead to questioning of how we relate to the world (Greene 1978).

Exploring Multiple Perspectives

A well-rounded education must include elements that promote an understanding of students' own backgrounds and cultures, and awareness that theirs is not the only perspective. Asking students to reflect on their backgrounds and what makes them who they are develops an awareness of where they come from. Often the sense of what has influenced them is so ingrained that they have lost the ability to see it without looking for it (Banks 1994; McIntosh 1990). This "monocultural" perspective leaves students thinking that there is one cultural system that everyone is part of. This notion blocks students from understanding others who are different from them. As McIntosh notes, "There is no culturally unmarked person" (3).

Participating in drama can allow students the opportunity to inhabit other perspectives, develop empathy, and develop the ability to understand the many vantage points that come into play in any situation. As students imagine they are characters, and envision themselves in particular environments and specific circumstances, they can act out different choices based upon their characters' frames of reference. Realizing that there are perspectives other than one's own is critical to success in a world that is ever more diverse and complex.

Drama integration can encourage cultural grounding for students and sensitize them to an awareness of otherness. This knowledge, once unearthed, creates an awareness of how powerfully their unique perspectives and backgrounds influence their responses to life issues. Students need to be aware that they carry assumptions about the world with them. Exploring their own set of assumptions provides students with a basis for understanding their own socio-cultural perspectives. Mattson (2008), reflecting on integrating drama in the study of history, notes, "(process-drama) also has the power to raise the stakes of critical historical anyalysis for young people, provoking students' cruiosity and inviting an emobdied form of critical primary document analysis" (103).

Describing the power of dramatic role-play, Doherty (1996) says, "Students are...offered the chance through improvised role-plays to rehearse, 'inhabit,' and 'voice' perspectives. Role-plays offer the possibility of sensitizing students to both their limits and capacities for understanding unfamiliar points of view" (157).

This investigation of what informs the decisions of a particular character leads to skills in empathy and understanding human behavior that foster better collaboration and leadership development. Rosler (2008) noticed that in an exploration of historical content in her fifth grade classroom in some cases her students' involvement, "went beyond mrere engagement, as they became active decision makers and leaders in the drama" (267).

Exploration of Ideas

Dramatic work activates students' thinking processes. It requires that knowledge and information be transformed. Students use their understanding of a situation and of a character to create new ground in a dramatic situation. They play with a fictional set of circumstances, investigating a diverse range of possibilities for human behavior. Drama develops the ability to think divergently, to imagine possibilities, and to test ways of responding to the world that equip them for success in a world that we can't yet imagine. Nellie McCaslin, in discussing the creative influence of drama, notes, "Creativity is the act of repatterning the known world into meaningful new configurations" (2000, 25).

Drama magnifies and explores sensitive issues by using metaphor to understand complex concepts (Goldberg and Phillips

1995; Parsons and Blocker 1993; Boal 1995; Schutzman and Cohen-Cruz 1994). It provides a lens for looking at problems and uncovering fresh perspectives.

Because drama has the ability to isolate situations and magnify moments and ideas, it provides the opportunity to tease out nuances of complex issues and concepts. It can provide distance, a safe space within which one can walk amidst the pieces of a complex puzzle, reflect, and consider while keeping emotion and personal agenda at bay. Teacher Kate DePalo noted, "I have already noticed that my classes are collaborating on a different level. They are dissecting information through exploration and as a result have been extremely intuitive, thoughtful, and engaged. I have found that through drama my students are building relationships and making connections with the material" (DePalo, pers. comm.).

Communication Fluency

Drama work calls upon students to use their full range of physical expression, to explore the nuances of verbal and non-verbal communication, and to become astute observers. Drama requires that students communicate both with words and without, developing an awareness of context and perspective and how this affects communication—in other words, how things are communicated and how they are received.

Think about how much there is to learn about effective communication. In addition to words, incorporating the details of speech that hold information—pauses, stutters, half-statements— adds unspoken meaning. Theater artist Normie Noel makes the point that it is important to consider all of these nuances because a quiet moment, pause, or false start can communicate more than a full sentence. The *way* in which we communicate, not just what we say, is loaded with meaning (Noel, pers. comm.). This knowledge is invaluable to students who are learning how to communicate effectively and that language is informed by context, inflection, and non-verbal communication.

Supporting Reading Comprehension

Research has shown that successful reading requires being able to enter into the world of the story. Drama can bolster comprehension of a story by allowing students to explore the story from inside and by physically embodying the story and its characters. When participating in drama, students create the meaning of the text through their words, both written and spoken; kinesthetically through the motion and positioning of their bodies; visually through their stance, and observation of others; emotionally through their feelings, often expressed in gesture, music, or writing; intrapersonally as they reflect; and interpersonally as they create shared meanings by reacting and responding to the dramatic actions of others (Wilhelm 2007).

This kind of learning moves beyond the simple understanding of a story. Rather, as David Booth says, "Drama encourages children not to be satisfied with immediate, simplistic solutions but to keep exploring, peeling away the layers that cloud the meaning, it can help develop the 'what if' element that must be brought to print if true reading is to occur" (Booth cited in Wilhelm and Edmiston 1998, 37). This kind of engagement brings deeper comprehension and connections to students' real lives. Because they have experienced a text in a multi-sensory way—physically, emotionally, and visually—their learning is deeper and retention is longer.

Unique connections and impressions of a story can provide a jumping off point for how we choose to understand a story. Through drama, we can explore the places where the listener connects with the story world. Middle school teacher, drama educator, and researcher Jeffrey Wilhelm (1998) says, "As a teacher, I invite students to imagine together, actively depicting characters, forces, or ideas, and to interact in these roles. An enactment may be cast in the past, the present, or the future, but always happens in the 'now of time.' This is relevant in education because through enactments, you can highlight and teach strategies of reading and learning, and help students create interpretations of text that reverberate with artistic, aesthetic, and metaphoric meanings" (8). These dramas draw on what students know from prior knowledge, and allow them to make sense of the text they are reading.

What is created in an enactment must fit what students know from the text and the world. Dramatic enactments make hidden processes of reading and learning visible, manipulatable, and open to evaluation and revision (Wilhelm 2007). Wilhelm's research demonstrates the role of dramatic enactments in helping students "to 'take on the participant stance' to participate in and visualize textual worlds, enlivening their engagement with text, and assisting them in creating meaning with text" (Beach et al. 2002, 164).

Critical Literacy: Investigating Texts

The most powerful effect of drama is the ability to engage students in imagining themselves in a role. Each role has a particular lens or frame of reference through which the world is seen. Donning the dramatic lens allows students to be comfortable moving between perspectives—their own and that of others. Looking at the same situation through these various lenses prompts an understanding that there are many interpretations of a particular story. Asking students then to consider who is telling the story creates a heightened awareness and questioning of texts. Wilhelm and Edmiston (1998) write that drama provides, "a way of making meaning of the world by learning to look inward to define the self; to imagine and enter the selfhood and perspectives of others; and...to look outward to critically read and converse with the world, open always to change and transformation and to working toward these transformations" (149).

The process of dramatic inquiry allows us to unpack and explore various aspects of the story. Not only does this deepen comprehension, but it also prompts the development of critical literacy, where texts are not accepted at face value but explored from a variety of access points. We often assume there is one interpretation of a story. This is, of course, not true and the story will change based upon the vantage point from which it's told. A dramatic investigation of a story might probe these questions:

- From whose perspective is the story told?

- Who are the voices represented?

- Which voices are missing?

- What are the relationships between characters?

- What is the context of the story?

- What choices are made by each character and why?

In the language arts classroom this kind of exploration will bring a heightened sense of characters' inner worlds and choices. In social studies it could lead to a questioning of who's telling the story and a consideration of how the story might be represented differently if told by another character.

Drama allows students to experience something at many levels—aesthetically, emotionally, intellectually, and analytically. It develops the ability to tune in, not just receive it, but activating students to think, rethink, analyze, evaluate, and identify the relevance of a text to their lives. What better way to develop literacy than by entering the world of the text, by becoming the characters you are reading about and understanding why they make the choices they do? Dramatic enactment can serve as a way to deepen reading skills in the traditional sense, including comprehension and the implications for critical literacy where students learn to question texts and assumptions, and not accept a text as the truth.

Supporting English Language Learners

How often have you had English language learners who struggle to learn because they are not yet comfortable with English? Through drama, students are provided opportunities that simulate reality so language exploration and learning occurs in context and can be framed in a safe environment where risk-taking is supported. Culturally responsive strategies, such as reader's theater, tableaux, improvisation, visualization, and pantomime explored in this chapter provide multiple points of access at different levels of language learning. Physical expression, vocal variety, spoken word, and writing to explore the academic language of social studies respond to the following: contextual clues, relationship and circumstance, and language as a way to engage socially. Rieg and Paquett (2009) note that, "Besides being 'fun' learning experiences for children, drama and movement have been proven to assist with developing decoding skills, fluency, vocabulary, syntactic knowledge, discourse knowledge, and metacognitive thinking" (148).

Introductory Activity: Tableaux

Asking students to portray a concept without using words will provide a challenge and stretch their thinking. Give students a word or concept and have them use their bodies to represent that concept visually in a still picture, or tableau. Younger students can create shapes for concrete ideas such as inanimate objects and animals. Older students can tackle more abstract concepts such as balanced equations (mathematics), democracy (social studies), oxymoron (literature), or velocity (science). This activity can be done anywhere, anytime, with no preparation or materials.

1. **Create Tableaux:** Give students a concept or vocabulary word and tell them they must use their bodies to create still shapes that represent that idea. Ask students to experiment with using different levels (placing their bodies in different positions at low, medium, and high levels) to make the image interesting. Once students have successfully explored the given concepts in single sculptures, you can move on to group tableaux that are more complex and show relationships between characters. Each group should identify a sculptor and the rest of the group will be the "clay" (Boal 2002).

2. **Gallery Walk:** Once students create their tableaux, you can ask them to create a caption or title for their image. This prompts students to move between image and text, which draws out new ideas. Have students decide whether they will reveal their caption before, after, or during the presentation of the image to viewers (each choice will yield a different result).

   Ask the class to imagine they are in a sculpture gallery and have a "gallery walk" in which each tableau is viewed as a sculpture. As the students examine each tableau, ask them to name aloud what they think is being depicted. Keep a list of the words students suggest, and discuss them later in relationship to the actual word.

   After the vocabulary word being sculpted is either identified or shared with the group, ask the sculptor and "clay" to discuss their creative process and what they learned during the activity.

3. **Tapping In:** After students create and view a sculpture, have an audience member "tap" a character or object to life. Ask the sculpted figure to share in a line or two what they might be thinking. By "tapping" characters/ideas/objects to life, the inner thinking process of a figure is revealed.

4. **Slide Show:** Move from vocabulary words to stories or sequenced concepts by asking students to create a series of tableaux to tell a story as in a slide show, where one image is shown right after the next. Each tableau should capture a snapshot of a moment in time. You can ask students who are viewing to close their eyes between each image by saying, "curtains down" (eyes shut) and "curtains up" (eyes open). This allows the groups who are creating an image to prepare their sculpture so the viewers see only the completed image.

Tableaux: Curriculum Connections

Tableaux can be used flexibly across content areas. In mathematics, students can create tableaux of where polygons appear in the world. Their peers guess both the items being portrayed and the contexts for the shapes. In science, students can create tableaux of mitosis and meiosis in a series of images like a "slide show" that reveals how cells divide. Each tableau "slide" has a caption that describes the moment. In social studies, students can depict a moment that might have occurred during the Boston Tea Party and colonists are tapped to life, each saying a line that reveals their inner thinking.

Drama Strategies

Once students are comfortable with creating tableaux, introduce new dramatic strategies for learning curricular content. Give students a starting place, such as a specific moment in history or literature, the beginning of a scientific process, or the point in a mathematical problem at which they must make a choice about how to proceed. The introduction to students of a scenario to explore can trigger a rich investigation framed by the characters, situation, context, and time period. Students bring the details to life through these strategies as the drama unfolds, allowing them to explore stories from the inside out.

Pantomime

"Pantomime is the art of conveying ideas without words" (McCaslin 2000, 71). Ask students to tell a story or show a concept through movement without using words. They can capture action, relationships, and the progression of a story without worrying about dialogue. Communicating ideas nonverbally will require students to think differently about the concepts they are portraying.

Improvisation

In improvisation, students build dramatic scenes by creating the drama in the moment, without reading from a script. Give students characters, a location, and time, and tell them to pretend they are the characters and let the drama unfold spontaneously.

This allows students to bring stories, historical moments, and concepts to life by applying their understanding of story, character, and motivation in their own language. This leads students to draw more fully on comprehension skills as they bring their understanding of a story into the improvised moment.

Mantle of the Expert

Mantle of the Expert, developed by drama educator Dorothy Heathcote, invites students to imagine that they are experts in the field being studied. Give students a role, such as a biologist who studies cell division or a historian who has written about the Civil War, and have the other students interview the "expert." This encourages students to take on a particular role and specific lens, which then deepens the research or investigation that is taking place. "The students inhabit their roles as experts in the enterprise with increasing conviction, complexity, and truth" (Heathcote and Bolton 1995, viii).

Monologue

A monologue is a moment in a play or story in which a character speaks without interruption by others. This can be an internal monologue in which the character is speaking to him- or herself (soliloquy), or it could be addressed to another character or to the audience. Have students select a character from history, literature, or a newspaper story and create a monologue, focusing on an issue that this character would be concerned about. Have students inhabit the character, consider his or her personal or professional stance, and think through these questions:

- What is the compelling story you want to tell or argument you want to make?

- What are you trying to persuade us about?

- What do you want (motivation)?

- What are the key themes or talking points you need to weave in to share your thinking?

- What is the emotional tone of what you're saying?

Drama Across the Curriculum

Here are some simple drama activities that can be used at any grade level. All are easy to implement in any classroom; learning through drama does not require elaborate sets or intricate costumes.

Drama in Language Arts

Becoming a character in a story and exploring a situation through drama deepens comprehension skills and the ability to visualize what is happening and understand characters' choices. Have students create a voice collage in which they read aloud a series of carefully selected character voices from a book. The juxtaposing voices should overlap, bringing multiple voices into a space exploring themes of the text. Students can create tableaux based on critical moments from texts, or write and perform short scenes as different characters.

In the Classroom

Middle school teachers in Maine devised an innovative approach for exploring a variety of moments in *The Phantom Tollbooth* (Juster 1988) text using tableaux. The entire class used the drama strategy of tableaux to create a life-size road map of Milo's trip. Not only did the living map retell Milo's trip, it showed the life lessons he learned along the way. At each place that he stopped the students created their tableau of who or what was there and morphed their human sculpture into the lesson that Milo learned.

Cindy Denny, a teacher in Alaska, used the book *Cindy Ellen: A Wild Western Cinderella* by Susan Lowell (2000) to work on word choice from a six-trait writing rubric. She asked her students to imagine that Cindy Ellen and the other characters from the book were invited to appear on the Dr. Phil Show. Students took on the roles of different characters and were interviewed by Dr. Phil and the audience (the rest of the class). Students discussed how getting into the role of various characters brings out "voice" and enriches and deepens understanding. They identified how various characters' voices were different and led to word choices. Students then went on to create a dramatization of an alternate ending to the book. Students edited their endings, then exchanged with another group for editing, working toward a final draft. Students then acted out their alternate endings in their small group.

Drama in Social Studies

Students often see history as being disconnected from their lives. Bring history to life by asking students to imagine that they are a person from times past. Have students explore the idea of monologue by writing a journal entry for a historical figure or imaginary person living in the time being studied. Or, have small groups of students act out pivotal moments in history, then explore how the scenes would have been different if alternate decisions had been made by the characters.

Have groups of students create pantomime and act out (without speaking) the character traits of a historical figure, showing the trait through movement. As each small group shares their pantomime, exemplifying one trait, have the rest of the class describe what they saw, generating a rich list of descriptions for the vocabulary being explored.

Once students have developed characters and explored a historical story through drama, you can "hot seat" a character by having students interview the character about his or her choices, beliefs, background, etc. Students are often amazed at the knowledge that a character can share about his or her life and circumstances. This develops and reveals comprehension in a deeply engaging way.

In the Classroom

Using selected voices from Civil War source documents, a teacher had her students create a rhythm machine. In this dramatic technique, one person goes to the center of the room and creates a rhythmical sound and motion (in this case real voices from source documents were used). Someone else joins the "machine," by bringing in a complementary sound and motion triggered by the first. Participants continue to build on until everyone is included. This exercise was adapted by juxtaposing voices of different figures in history. The effect was remarkable as voices that represented perspectives from all walks of life—slave, plantation owner, newspaper reporter, conductor on the underground railroad, politician— were brought to life through voice and gesture.

Drama in Mathematics

Invite students to imagine that they have been hired to create an advertisement showing why the world needs geometry. Students should create a slogan, such as "Got Math?" and short informational segments on the use of geometric principles. This activity engages students in making sense of mathematical ideas, relating these ideas to real life, and using their own language and creativity to share the ideas. Students' series of commercials can then be performed for other classes.

Have students dramatize word problems, inviting them to invent characters and situations to make the problems more engaging. Allow them to use crazy props and costume pieces to flesh out the scenarios. They can invite the audience to calculate at key moments in the drama.

Drama in Science

Drama can allow students to enact scientific ideas through simulation such as the relationship between organelles and cellular structure, or scientific processes such as imagining a heart is a character reflecting on his/her role in the body through a monologue (Odegard 2003). Or, engage students in taking on the role of a scientist (Mantle of the Expert) and working through a scientific study. You might consider dramatizing moments of scientific discovery such as the discovery of the X-ray, to consider how scientific thinking and processes yield results, and build an awareness of how progress is made.

Ask students to take on the Mantle of the Expert on a scientific subject. Tell the "experts" that they need to review and interpret bar charts and graphs on the most current temperature statistics and draw inferences based on what the data say, then present their findings in a monologue.

In the Classroom

A kindergarten teacher asked her students to imagine they were scientists examining bones that she had created from paper maché. Based on the examination of bones through their observations and critical thinking, the junior scientists decided whether the bones belonged to a land dweller, sea dweller, or air dweller. The conversation held between the scientists revealed their scientific reasoning and understanding of the content.

Combining Drama With Other Art Forms

Have students use drama strategies to perform works in other art forms such as stories, poems, and music. Dramatize poetry by giving small groups different stanzas and asking the groups to perform the text through drama. Students can bring their own interpretations to bear through inventive choices—the repetition of lines, addition of characters, pantomimed movement, choral voices, and solo voices. Use storytelling to introduce a dramatic activity by offering a context or situation that can then be explored more fully through the development of scenes. Have students incorporate music into drama to create a mood, represent a character, heighten awareness, or punctuate moments.

Assessment

When assessing students' learning through drama, look at their use of dramatic process and presentation, as well as the content area concepts they are working with. Develop a checklist or rubric of content you are looking for and share it with students before they begin. Figure 4.1 shows a rubric for a monologue about scientific forces, which allows the teacher to assess both drama and content area learning as well as note unexpected outcomes.

Figure 4.1 Assessment Rubric for Monologue in Science

Assignment: Create a monologue in which you play the part of a physical force (electromagnetic, gravitational, nuclear, etc.) and convey your understanding of that force in relation to other forces.

Student Role:

Skill or Concept	Shows Deep Understanding	Shows Understanding	Shows Limited Understanding	Notes
Creatively portrays the point of view of a physical force	Portrays creative, engaging point of view of a physical force using facts, concepts, and original ideas	Portrays factually correct point of view of physical force	Does not portray point of view of physical force or portrays in factually incorrect manner	
Science standard: Knows that nuclear forces are much stronger than electromagnetic forces, which are vastly stronger than gravitational forces	Directly and creatively compares to other forces using facts, concepts, and original ideas	Compares to other forces using correct facts and concepts	Does not compare to other forces or compares incorrectly	
Uses body position, gesture, and tone of voice to convey understanding	Creative, engaging use of position and voice	Interesting use of position and voice	Static body position and monotone voice	

After students share their dramatic work, debrief with both the actors and the student audience using questions that are linked back to objectives. Discuss how students worked with content, how they decided to integrate the ideas, and how their thinking evolved. This makes the process visible, providing valuable evidence for how and where the learning unfolded for different learners in your class. Record notable student responses and use them as formative or summative assessment, depending on your goals. Questions might include the following:

- What ideas from our unit of study are explored in this work?

- What information is conveyed?

- What perspective(s) are we seeing represented? How do you know?

- What choices were made in creating the drama?

- What do you notice about the use of space/levels?

- What do you notice about relationships embedded in the scene?

- What information and ideas do you take away from viewing/experiencing this dramatic work?

Concluding Thoughts

Drama integration allows students to connect with curricular content in ways that develop ownership and imagination. Students make their thinking visible as they become characters, improvise scenes, and embody stories. As students examine the role of stories in history, science, and literature, they can understand themselves better and, at the same time, develop the ability to value a multitude of perspectives. Using their imagination and critical thinking skills, students learn through active engagement, improve their communication skills, and develop their own sense of voice.

Drama also allows students to enjoy the process of learning. Teacher Kate DePalo describes what she notices happening as drama comes into her classroom. "They are internalizing conflicts, problem solving, and are becoming more involved in the material being taught. Most importantly, I have noticed that these drama strategies have brought the essence of play into my classroom. My students are not only learning, but they are having a blast doing it" (DePalo, pers. comm.).

Through drama we can give our young people the time and space to learn the lessons of life without the risk of making grave mistakes with irretrievable results, and the unique chance to step outside of their personal frames of reference to understand how others think, feel, and react. A powerful connection between people and issues can be created in this space. Placing students as characters in fictional scenarios can provide them with opportunities for authentic responses that help them to understand how people change and develop in response to their circumstances (O'Neill and Lambert 1991). Drama integration can help students of all ages locate their personal voice and ultimately their identity.

Reflection

1. Where in your curriculum would exploring different perspectives deepen learning or create empathy?

2. How might embodying a character allow students to experience a story or historical moment from the inside out?

3. Choose one drama strategy described in this chapter. How could you integrate this strategy into your existing curriculum?

Chapter 5

Visual Art: Accessing Content Through Image

What Is Visual Art?

It's nearly impossible to find a succinct, shared definition of art. Lansing (2004) captures the dilemma in pinning down the idea of art in one definition, noting, "The popular view was, and continues to be, that art cannot be defined. Most artists and art educators hold to this view as some people hold to their religion. Art cannot be defined, they say, because the things we have called art do not all have a distinctive feature in common. If they did, we could say that any new work containing that feature is a work of art, and any work without that feature is not a work of art."

Often the question "What is art?" or "What is art for?" is posed to engage students in considering the full range of possible answers. Eric Booth, in his book *The Everyday Work of Art*, drew from the etymology of the word, offering the idea of "art" as both noun and verb. He notes, "At the birth of the word 'art,' it was a verb that meant to 'put things together.' It was not a product but a process" (1999, 5). In this chapter, we consider how putting images together can provide new ways to construct meaning.

Why Does Visual Art Matter?

We experience the world through images. We see and read images before we read words. For these reasons, the visual arts are a natural fit in the classroom as an approach to many subjects. Reading is enhanced by the creation of mental images. We often see students who are stumped about what to write; yet when they engage with images, suddenly their writing becomes filled with ideas and rich details. Science is dependent on observation. In mathematics, visualizing patterns is key. The use of images in the classroom creates a way to translate, communicate, and draw from the world. As you think about your next lesson, why not begin with looking? (Vivian Poey, pers. comm.)

There is growing data showing that visual arts improve academic achievement. In *Critical Links: Learning in the Arts and Student Academic and Social Development* (Deasy 2002), researchers found that engaging in visual arts allowed readers to visualize and interpret text and engaged readers more fully in content. *Teaching Literacy Through Art* (Korn 2012), a study conducted by the Guggenheim Museum, found that visual arts education enhanced literacy skills. "The study found that students in the program performed better in six categories of literacy and critical thinking skills—including thorough description, hypothesizing, and reasoning—than did students who were not in the program" (Kennedy 2006). Hetland et al. (2007), in their study *Studio Thinking: The Real Benefits of Visual Arts Education*, identified eight "studio habits of mind" developed by students taking arts classes: develop craft, engage and persist, envision, express, observe, reflect, stretch and explore, and understand the art world. Clearly students can benefit by working with visual art in the classroom, learning skills and knowledge in both visual arts and the curricular content being explored.

Common Core

Visual Learning in the Common Core State Standards

Visual literacy is an integral part of the Common Core State Standards. By responding to text in visual representations, students will make logical inferences from text, determine central ideas or themes, and interpret words and phrases (particularly figurative meanings), as stated in the Anchor Standards for Reading. Students will also integrate and evaluate content presented in visual formats and text. Through visual art, students can show their understanding of complex literary and informational texts. When critiquing their own visual work or the work of others, students will express their ideas clearly and persuasively, build on others' ideas, present supporting evidence, and evaluate information presented visually, as stated in the Anchor Standards for Speaking and Listening.

Observation and Interpretation of Visual Images

Every curricular theme has a visual aspect to it. Students can draw from the visual world to enhance what is being studied in the school curriculum. Visuals are open-ended in ways words are not and can prompt students to notice and make meaning. There is a lot of information embedded in an image, and this can add to and deepen classroom investigations. Working with images in this way will inevitably enhance writing. If you think about it, description is a visual thing. By working with visuals, students' writing will have access to rich details and characteristics of the image (Robert Shreefter, pers. comm.).

Observation is central to working with visual art. Begin with visual narrative and then move into language narrative. Create images and ask students to add words. This allows students to draw on their own observations. Observation is contextual by nature, so situating the image in the context of the curriculum being studied makes a difference (Robert Shreefter, pers. comm.).

Production of Visual Images

When students are allowed to select from a variety of materials and use the elements of art to convey meaning, making art can be a form of active learning and a way of synthesizing ideas, as well as a form of assessment as they "show what they know." Provide students with opportunities to explore a range of art materials and processes to create their own images. Offer direct experiences with paint, clay, drawing tools, photographs, textured papers, and other media. As students make choices about how they use materials to communicate, they use higher-order thinking skills such as analysis and evaluation. Students think about how best to work with materials at hand to represent an idea visually.

Students work with the elements of visual art—line, form, shape, color, texture, and pattern—to make meaning and construct ideas. There are choices to be made about why this color, or why that kind of line (Vivian Poey, pers. comm.). As students create, they draw information from a range of sources and use the elements of art to express their ideas about that information. The elements of art are tools with which students construct meaning. Students learn about the elements as they create.

Visual representation is applicable to every content area. Students can use clay to construct vessels built from geometric shapes, learn about perimeter through sculpture, and tie visual arts to math goals by making abstract concepts concrete. Comprehension and descriptive writing can be enhanced as students create storyboards that show the progression of a fairytale they are creating. Moving between image and text as students represent their understanding of significant moments in the story can enrich the descriptive details used as students draw ideas from their paintings. Students are called upon to use their imaginations to create new ideas, use materials in a two- or three-dimensional space to communicate those ideas, and show that they have met developmental benchmarks and curricular standards.

Visual arts experiences allow students to use art as their own language. Because there are no formulaic rules, as there are in writing, visual art allows kids who do not draw well or who do not yet have knowledge of the elements of art to participate. The trick for the teacher is to ease students into using their imaginations, to allow them to understand that trial and error is a natural part of the process, and that art is a mode of expression that is defined by each individual student.

How is what is in their heads different from what they finally come up with? Often there is a "happy accident" or a difference between what was planned and how it came out. Art can be exciting because students do not know what they are going to get; it is new. In visual arts, it is the making itself that is key (Robert Shreefter, pers. comm.). The creative process allows students to work from the same instructions but present their learning through different interpretations. In this way, students learn from each other and bring forward their own unique translations while demonstrating their content learning.

Introductory Activity: Storyboarding

Here is an introductory lesson to get students thinking visually in which students create a series of images based on curricular content. Tell students that they will be creating a storyboard to share ideas about a concept. This could include a sequential story (beginning, middle, end), the description of a scientific process (chemical reaction, the path of the circulatory system, or growth of a seed into a plant), or the factors that lead up to a historical moment. Working from images allows students to first work metaphorically, and writing will be more richly descriptive as a result.

1. **Planning Sketch:** Decide how many panels students will need to create a visual narrative. Fold and then unfold large newsprint paper so that the folds create square or rectangular sections for sketches. Ask students to use the newsprint panels as a place to develop ideas and sketch rough thumbnail images in pencil that can be fully developed in the final storyboard. Note that the planning process requires different skills than actually implementing ideas. They are not replicating content twice. Rather, they are identifying and developing ideas on newsprint, and then manifesting the fully developed ideas in the final storyboard. Ask students in their planning phase to experiment with layout so that they are thinking about how they are using the space in each panel.

2. **Storyboard:** Once students have created a draft of the storyboard, they can use that plan to create their final product. At this point, they can add words to the images. This prompts students to move between image and text, which draws out new ideas. Give students choices of how they want to depict their visual narrative; not all students are comfortable drawing. Offer students a choice of taking photographs, using images from online sources or magazines, painting abstract shapes, or using found materials to create a collage. The focus should be on conveying a sequence of ideas.

3. **Sharing:** Ask students to share their storyboards, discussing what they've created, what they learned in the process, the choices they made, and how they are investigating the curricular concept.

4. **Feedback:** Ask the rest of the class to talk about what they see in the storyboards that is interesting or made them think, and how they are similar to or different from choices they have made (Robert Shreefter, pers. comm.).

The sequencing of visual images is an organizing and idea-generating strategy for more structured writing activities as well. Teacher Stacy Winterfeld notes, "I have learned…that struggling writers may benefit from creating storyboards prior to writing their ideas down on paper. By first creating and viewing images, they then may be more successful in developing the words and sentences needed to describe what they want to say…. By sketching out their ideas, we are allowing our students a much higher chance of success and creativity with their writing, while also allowing them to potentially dig much deeper and think much more critically than they may otherwise have been doing."

Visual Arts Strategies

There are many ways to introduce visual arts into your curriculum. Here are a few flexible, easy-to-implement strategies.

Visual Essay

Assign or allow students to choose a curricular concept and allow time for students to find related images from a variety of sources: Internet, magazines, photocopies from books, etc. Then, have students choose and sequence the images to tell a story. Students can add language or writing to the presentation of images. Have students create an exhibit of their visual works, create books, or present their images in a blog or website. Encourage students to look analytically at each image, questioning what is noticeable and what is not. Have students present their visual essays to the group to look, discuss, and describe what is there, or what is suggested.

Observational Drawing

Observational drawing is a heightened way of observing. Have students closely observe items related to a curricular area of study, such as leaves, rocks, or flowers (science), tessellations or Mandelbrot sets (mathematics), or historical artifacts or art (social studies), and ask them to draw what they see. The focus is less on getting a beautiful drawing and more on close observation as long as students are representing details that they observe. Working visually cultivates the development of deep observation skills, and an interest in noticing detail. This attention to detail can then translate into students' writing.

"When you draw, you learn to see the world completely differently. Sketches allow you to notice closely and document details. You realize that the world is not made out of lines, that white is not white—it's purple or green and it changes when the light hits. Asking students to document their learning visually can allow students to focus in on details, and discover based on their own observations" (Vivian Poey, pers. comm.).

Collage

Provide students with a variety of collage materials (textured material, colored paper, origami paper, found objects such as leaves, etc.) and have students construct visual representations of curricular concepts. Encourage students to experiment with different ways to put the materials together, considering color, shape, textures, and meaning. Have students observe what others have done, which will spark new ideas for their own work. Hold a discussion of each other's work, and have students respond in oral language or writing.

Mixed Media

Invite students to work with a range of media, such as clay, paint, colored pencils, etc., to produce visual work based on curricular content. These materials can provide students with new ways to create a visual response to content, to represent their understanding of an idea, or to investigate a concept as an exploration.

Visual Arts Across the Curriculum

Like all the arts, visual arts are flexible enough to be used across the curriculum. Between testing and worksheets, you may worry that there is not time for this kind of in-depth work. Yet, there are ways to structure your classroom to integrate the visual arts to deepen learning. Show visual images to students to provide context, or provoke discussion in a unit. Ask students to express their understanding in a visual response. Have students keep visual journals with sketches, cut out images, and photographs to demonstrate their ideas and to stimulate writing. You will find that for many students, working visually enhances their writing with more descriptive language. Hubbard (1987) argues, "Children's drawings are viable tools for problem solving. Through them children make sense of the world, and impart their visions. Teachers who channel children narrowly toward verbal solutions may be denying them the opportunity to share the full power of their images" (60).

Visual Arts in Mathematics

Many students struggle with the study of mathematics. Incorporating visual imagery into your math lessons can help make mathematical concepts more tangible. For example, kindergarten and first grade students can work on number concepts by drawing addition and subtraction story problems or creating them through sculpture. Cut sponges or potatoes into geometric shapes and have students dip them into paint and stamp repeating patterns such as AB, ABAB, or ABCABC. This helps make an abstract math concept concrete and can illustrate student learning (Susan Fisher, pers. comm.). Have older students explore the idea of symmetry by creating tessellations, designs where a shape is repeated to form a pattern. This can be done using pen and ink on paper or through collage in which students must paste shapes together on the picture plane in symmetrical balance. This activity requires students to plan and measure carefully and solve practical mathematical problems (Bellisario, pers. comm.). Check out a library book on folding origami and have students create origami animals to investigate angles and fractions. A lotus fold for instance, the basis for most origami, is folded in half, then quarters, and then eighths.

A more complex activity can address multiple standards at once. Have students create a self-portrait soft sculpture puppet. Have students create their own rulers, use them to measure in the initial planning stages, and use a protractor to find the circumference of a circle, which becomes the pattern for the puppet head. Then have students determine the radius of the circle and weigh out stuffing on a scale. Have students document their thinking and creative process in a work portfolio. Display the puppets along with students' written explanations of the mathematical concepts. In addition to providing a hands-on and engaging entry into the study of mathematics, this lesson allows for meaningful dialogue with students about their own abilities and how math concepts are used in their lives (Creegan-Quinquis, pers. comm.).

Visual Arts in Science

Observation is key to scientific understanding. Use visual arts as a way to focus and expand student observations. Have students observe and draw scientific processes. For example, have students plant seeds and document in images what they notice at each stage of growth, as well as what they imagine will happen next. To kick off a study of light, have students paint the sky at different times of the day—observing and documenting what they see in paint.

Begin a unit of study with deep observation (Poey, pers. comm.). Focus on observation by asking students to create a drawing of an object, and then use a viewfinder (a square cut out of paper) to zoom in their subject. Have students draw or paint the smaller, detailed view, noticing finer details, color, and value. Then have students zoom in even more and transform what they see into abstract shapes as if they were looking through a microscope. Have students create a science newsletter featuring these drawings and students' writings about the progression of their looking (Kerrie Bellisario, pers. comm.).

This focus on deepening observational skills can be transferred to different areas of science. Have students keep a nature journal, first sketching what they see in the environment, then describing their observations in text. Middle school students can use a visual journal to track their discoveries during dissection labs.

Visual art integration also involves making more visible to students the fact that the visual arts have always been involved in the other disciplines. Painting involves understanding the chemistry of pigments and chemicals to achieve colors, photography involves the chemical components of developing a picture, and drawing and painting involve preparing raw materials as well as measurement, perspective, and patterning (Susan Fisher, pers. comm.). Use real-world science in the visual arts as a means to explore scientific concepts.

The materials used to create visual art can provide hands-on experience with scientific principles. Watercolors are clean and easy to work with to explore cause and effect. Just put a dollop of watercolor from a tube on a plate and let it dry—this will give you enough paint to use for two lessons. Allow students to experiment with laying down crayon color and painting watercolor over it (wax resist). Have students sprinkle salt onto wet watercolors where it will crystallize and create patterns. Have students observe and document these changes and processes closely and then use students' experiences as an introduction to the scientific principles involved. These experiments can also enhance learning in the visual arts. When students are allowed to play with materials, they discover new possibilities and then use this information when creating compositions (Susan Fisher, pers. comm.).

Visual arts can also be a synthesizing activity and a form of assessment in science. Have students create a photomontage of scientific processes such as decay or states of matter. Have them apply their research of habitat by creating pop-up books that illustrate the flora and fauna that exist in different geographic zones. Visual representations of understanding can serve as a great assessment tool to show what students have learned in their research.

Visual Arts in Social Studies

Observing art (photographs, painting, collage, sculpture, carvings, etc.) can serve as a jumping off point for discussions about an era, a movement, or a culture. Viewing exemplars of work that artists have created can be a great way to set the stage for work in the classroom. These artists can inspire and serve as examples of people who create, but their work also provides ways into writing and research. Mural artist Judy Baca, for example, works with historical traditions in mural making, drawing from the community for inspiration. Installation artist Fred Wilson creates museum installations that question who is represented and who is not. Collage artist Romare Bearden documents the areas where he lived and worked, capturing African American culture in the 1930s. Viewing artist exemplars can spark student projects that allow them to engage in similar explorations through visual mediums.

Free resources, such as government photo archives, provide a wealth of visual information. For example, the Works Progress Administration (WPA) and the Farm Security Administration (FSA) put unemployed artists to work during the Great Depression to document every facet of American life, resulting in one of the largest photo collections in the world, available online for free through the Library of Congress website.

Students can create visual works based on their own lives as well. Have students create neighborhood maps, including where they live and three different places of interest. Then, have students map out their paths to get from one place to another. Students should use different lines, textures, and colors to represent different areas of their maps.

In the Classroom

Visual arts can help students make personal connections to curriculum. A former fifth grade sheltered English teacher in Boston used an arts-based approach to biography/autobiography writing that attempts to build a direct bridge from the biography of a character from early American history to students' lives. Each student created a book illustrating a significant moment in the life of an historical American figure. The art provided language for representing this moment. These turning points reflected students' own diverse experiences and journeys. For example, one student chose Squanto learning English, which was parallel to his own learning of a new language. Another student chose Sacajawea's entering another culture, which mirrored the student's own journey. Students selected one event in their character's life to depict in a pop-up book. Deepening their knowledge about one event supported students in constructing timelines—a string of events in a life. Students placed their biography timelines on a larger timeline of American history. They paired up with Timeline Buddies for discussion throughout the writing process.

The teacher reflected on how students worked collaboratively: "One student quickly became our tree expert, teaching others; another was an expert at drawing the figure; and yet another, at some of the engineering skills necessary for making 3-D work and conceptualizing one scene in three rows of the book. Concepts such as foreground, mid-ground, background as well as scale and grounding elements, etc., were considered.

Text-illustration congruence was also discussed. Some of the students' moments were really a period in a figure's life. How could a student choose only one moment—and which moment would be most crucial to represent? Our biographer of Squanto asked the class for help. Should he have Squanto sitting at a desk learning English? Or should Squanto, now having learned English, be addressing his people? After much consideration, Squanto was to be placed on the deck of the ship to represent his leaving London to return to America. This solution not only pinpointed this moment but it spoke to his time in England, his need to return to America, and symbolized the great journey he had taken. This and other discussions became the key aspect in having students collaborate, learn about each other's figures, and piece together strategies for both easy and very complex issues of representation and use of symbols" (Donovan, Shreefter, and Adams 2005).

Visual Arts in Language Arts

Often students are hesitant to write because they feel unsuccessful as writers. Visual arts for many students do not create the same angst. Working in the visual arts allows students to create and decode another type of language—to create metaphors that reflect their ideas and understanding. Students can create images that stand for particular ideas that are symbolic and they can discover what happens when they move from image to text. Coming up with an image first is often easier than writing cold (Robert Shreefter, pers. comm.). Conversely, when students are asked to write first and then translate the ideas from their writing into visual images, they are analyzing text, problem solving, and making critical decisions as they decide what images to use (Kerrie Bellisario, pers. comm.).

Begin by asking students to maintain a visual journal, in which they keep observational sketches. Shreefter says that when students begin to think using both languages (visual and written), both benefit. He notes, "The creation of art allows students to create their own language for expressing who they are and what they know. They can use classroom texts along with their own languages and experiences for writing and art making" (Robert Shreefter, pers. comm.). Have students create visual essays on any topic of study or have them create books to visually document their personal ideas about curricular content or their lives.

In the Classroom

Maureen Creegan-Quinquis uses a process-based art integration approach to the teaching of writing that builds upon the work of Susan Sheridan. Sheridan suggests that teachers can use blind contour drawing as an entry point into writing, which can be particularly useful for English language learners (Sheridan 1997, 5).

The blind contour technique asks students to draw without looking, critiquing, or erasing the drawing, preventing students from being paralyzed with self-consciousness and preventing too much self-critiquing as they draw. In this technique the drawing is not analyzed as it is created, which facilitates a smoother translation from what the student observes to what is put on the paper.

Creegan-Quinquis asks students to draw a natural artifact, such as a leaf, in pencil without looking at what they are drawing until it is finished. As students draw the leaf without looking at the lines they are making, focusing fully on the leaf as they draw, they are asked to think about how they would describe the marks they have made. Is the line smooth? Is the edge of the leaf wiry? Students are asked to note the type of lines that emerge. When they are finished drawing, they write words that describe the lines they have made. In doing this, they are cataloguing visual information.

Students then work in pairs or in small groups to compare and discuss their word choices. They begin with words they feel they can use for an entry into writing and then work with each other to expand the vocabulary. These new vocabulary words and descriptors can become seeds for poetry, stories, or other writings.

Assessment

Critique is a natural part of making art. Students should be given opportunities to self-assess as well as engage in dialogue about their work with their instructor and peers. This can lead to teachable moments as students' sharing of their work draws out realizations and observations (Vivian Poey, pers. comm.). Have student artists show their work and ask questions that encourage divergent thinking. What do you see? What do you like about this? What meaning do you see in the images? In these discussions, introduce the vocabulary of visual arts, such as scale, line, shape, color, form, texture, and pattern. As students discuss their work, record or keep notes on student insights or statements that show what they have learned about the process.

Guide discussion so that you can assess what students are learning. Ask questions that draw out knowledge and observation from both the viewers and the creator to deepen the learning experience. For the viewers, guide their looking to help them articulate what they see. Notice the aspects of the piece: color, shape, line, and object. Ask questions such as:

- What do you see?

- What don't you see?

- What does it make you think of?

- How does it make you feel?

- What is communicated about the ideas in our unit?

- How are the ideas represented?

Next, question the artist who created the work to draw out his or her process. Ask questions, such as:

- What choices did you as the artist make in the development of your work? Why?

- What did you learn by translating content ideas into visual form?

- Did the viewers see something unexpected or unintended in your work? Why do you think that is?

The fact that each student produces something different through his or her own interpretation of the content is important. Looking closely at each other's work and understanding the artists' choices are part of the art-making process. Shreefter explains, "Techniques can also be discussed in context. 'When would you make the colors not be realistic? Why?' This is a different kind of learning where students have more control of knowledge and how they work with it" (Robert Shreefter, pers. comm.).

The visual arts offer a powerful option for assessing students' content knowledge. Students can use drawings to show what they know about plant growth, create collages to represent historical themes, or produce sculptures to show their mastery of geometry concepts. From this, you can see what students have learned and how they have interpreted the information. Have students explain their artistic process verbally or in written form.

Provide students with a list or rubric of content standards that they will be responsible for conveying in their visual work, as well as expectations about their artistic representations. Use a rubric or rating scale to assess final work. Figure 5.1 shows a rating scale for a visual arts project in social studies.

Figure 5.1 Visual Arts in Social Studies Rating Scale

Assignment: Create a visual representation of developments in the English, French, and Spanish colonies in North America.

Skill	Circle Level
Historical Understanding standard: Knows how to construct and interpret multiple tier time lines (e.g., a time line that compares developments in the English, French, and Spanish colonies in North America)	1 Basic 2 Proficient 3 Advanced
Selects materials thoughtfully and uses them to convey meaning. Materials used:	1 Basic 2 Proficient 3 Advanced
Uses the elements of art effectively. Elements used:	1 Basic 2 Proficient 3 Advanced
Explains thinking and process clearly.	1 Basic 2 Proficient 3 Advanced
Notes:	

In the Classroom

Leah Jaeks, a kindergarten teacher in Green Bay, Wisconsin, taught a unit on the ocean. She constructed a visual art pre- and post-assessment to assess her students' learning. For the pre-test, Jaeks introduced some basic art instruction, discussing line, shape, and form and demonstrating how to mix colors. She then asked her students to create a painting of the ocean, including as many details as they could think of. This work allowed Jaeks to assess students' prior knowledge about the oceans. After the unit of study, she asked students to make another painting of the ocean and to include as many details as they could think of. What she had expected to find in the assessment differed from what she actually learned.

"I thought the students would have automatically added more ocean life to their end-of-unit painting. Some did, but most added more detail and worked on the technique of using watercolors. They experimented in mixing colors and adding more or less paint for emphasis. When they described their end-of-unit paintings, their ocean vocabulary increased and in some cases their creativity did as well. So, I expected more quantity of ocean life in their final paintings, but what I observed was better quality paintings and their ocean vocabulary had increased when they described their paintings." By using visual arts as an assessment, Jaeks was able to tease out what the children had learned and also discovered an increase in vocabulary.

Concluding Thoughts

Encouraging students to explore ideas through the making of images allows them to tap into ideas, feelings, and responses that may be elusive in written or spoken word at first try. King and Ippolito (2001) argue that "Linguistic knowledge cannot completely explain or describe what we know, and trying to verbalize our thoughts and feelings frequently obstructs the self-discovery process" (71). Drawing and the creation of images allow students to explore their ideas in new forms. As Karen Gallas (1991) reflected on the use of drawing as a way of understanding insects in her classroom, "Knowing wasn't just telling something back as we had received it. Knowing meant transformation and change.... For both children and teacher, the arts offer opportunities for reflection upon the content and the process of learning and they foster a deeper level of communication about what knowledge is and who is truly in control of the learning process" (50). Allowing students to move between "languages" of text and image provides new ways for students to explore, relate to, and express ideas.

The fact that each student produces something different through his or her own interpretation of the content is important. Looking closely at each other's work and appreciating the choices are part of the art-making process. It allows everyone in the classroom to appreciate the work, rather than evaluating based on a hierarchical idea of the right answer. "When we use our own experience...I learn about you, you learn about me or about the students in the first row. The other way we always assume the teacher has the answer and that we have to find out what it is. One of the things about art-making and about appreciation of other art is just that. We become appreciators rather than people who know or don't know. We become people who are excited about learning about and from each other, even if we don't agree. Which is a lot different from not knowing the answers" (Robert Shreefter, pers. comm.). This is a different kind of learning where students have more control of knowledge and how they work with it.

148

Reflection

1. Where might the use of illustration heighten observation skills in your curriculum?

2. What artist exemplars might serve as catalysts to deepen a curricular topic?

3. When students work with different materials (paint, clay, oil sticks, found objects), how does the way they express their ideas change?

Chapter 6

Creative Movement as a Learning Process

[F]rom infancy onwards we interpret the world not just intellectually, but through our senses, our physical intelligence.

—Grove, Stevens, and McKechnie (2005, 4)

Children are natural movers. When asked to sit for long periods of time, their brains disconnect. Fidgeting begins... minds wander. Bringing movement into the classroom stimulates brain activity, preparing students for deeper learning throughout the day. As Susan Griss, choreographer, teaching artist, and Lesley University Creative Arts in Learning adjunct faculty member, notes, "Children naturally move. They react to and explore the world in physical ways. No one has to teach them to jump for joy, to roll down a grassy hill, or to pound their bodies on the floor during a tantrum. When they arrive in elementary school, they are fluent in this nonverbal, physical language.

However, rather than using this natural resource by channeling it into constructive learning experiences, teachers often expend energy subduing children's physicality…. What if, instead, teachers used kinesthetic language to teach elementary curricular subjects?" (Griss 1998, 1). Learning is not confined to our head. Movement is learning, exploration, and investigation.

We are constantly "reading" and interpreting body language as part of how we communicate, but often this is not a skill that is developed intentionally. In addition to activating learning, students also benefit from developing their understanding of how they communicate using nonverbal language. Brownfeld (2010) argues that verbal language, which includes "speaking, listening, reading, and writing," is one way of communicating, but we also draw heavily on our ability to read and communicate in nonverbal language. She adds, "Though each type of language can function effectively in their respective arenas, communication can occur on a deeper level if both communicative forms are used together" (8). Brownfeld advocates for education not only to connect to students' minds, but to become an embodied process, that, quoting from Liz Lerman, "uses the body and the body's internal and external awarenesses as a partner in acquiring knowledge, assuaging curiosity, and pursuing being a human being" (Lerman in Brownfeld 2010, 10).

This chapter considers the possibilities for integrating creative movement across the curriculum to investigate curricular topics.

What Is Creative Movement?

In creative movement, students make movement choices about how they will use their bodies to express ideas and concepts. In the classroom, creative movement can be applied to curriculum material students are studying. From the solar system to mathematical equations, from the journeys of the Underground Railroad to the transformation of caterpillars to butterflies, creative movement has applications across curriculum and grade levels. As such, it is a powerful tool for connecting curriculum concepts to personal expression and experience, providing a rich and unforgettable educational experience for students. It does not require pre-training in movement or a particular physical ability. Creative movement draws from the innate human ability to communicate through movement (Miller and Glover 2010).

You might be wondering—what's the difference between movement in drama (pantomime) and creative movement? Creative movement is more abstract than movement in drama. The focus is on the movement itself, not on pretending to move like an animal, plant, or character. Minton (2003) notes that creating movement pieces "involves connecting movements together to produce short pieces of movement or sequences, and ultimately shaping these sequences" (39).

Creative movement is not about learning "steps" or "moves." It is "about using the thinking tools of dance to create and build analogical and metaphoric connections between embodied experience and curriculum content. These interpretations are at once expressive and intellectual, individual and collaborative" (Celeste Miller, pers. comm.).

Why Does Creative Movement Matter?

Like other forms of artistic exploration, creative movement can be used as an inventive approach to investigate specific curricular content, to express understanding, and to explore ideas. Creative movement "also connects us to our body and this connection, often ignored, allows us to investigate intuitive honing and to begin to understand ourselves in relationship to ideas" (Bartholomew, pers. comm.). This form of embodied learning is how many students learn best.

The Mind-Body Connection

Bringing movement into the curriculum will benefit all learners by engaging their entire system for learning. "Movement awakens and activates many of our mental capacities. Movement integrates and anchors new information and experience into our neural networks, and movement is vital to all the actions by which we embody and express our learning, our understanding, and ourselves" (Hannaford 2005, 107).

Too often learning is treated as a "disembodied process" (Hannaford 2005, 15). Claudia Cornett (2003) notes that students benefit from integrating brain and body because, when the body is engaged, more parts of the brain are activated. Jensen (2001) confirms this connection between mind and body, saying that movement can "activate far more brain areas than traditional seatwork" (72). Griss elaborates, "Watch a group of healthey children at play. No doubt they will be moving. Even without hearing their words you will probably know what's going on by watching their activity, their body language, their physical energy dynamics. Children use their bodies to play, communicate, and express emotions" (Griss 1998, 1).

Brain researchers are discovering that incorporated movement and other senses are solidifying learning by supporting the development of neural pathways (Zull 2002). Biologist Carla Hannaford (2005) describes the way left and right brain functions can work together through movement. She says, "The logic hemisphere (usually the left hemisphere) tends to deal with details, the parts and processes of language and linear patterns. By contrast, the gestalt (usually the right hemisphere)—meaning whole processing or global as compared to linear—tends to deal with images, rhythm, emotion, and intuition" (90). The goal is to have the hemispheres work together in integrated thinking. She goes on to say that "the more we access both hemispheres, the more intelligently we are able to function" (91). Movement, then, can "anchor thought and build the skills with which we express our knowledge" (17).

The brain is constantly creating and connecting neural pathways. This neural plasticity allows the brain to learn and relearn. Hannaford (2005) discusses "the role of movement and play in activating" neural pathways, noting that there is a deep connection between body and mind that can enhance these neural pathways. She says, "Movement activates the neural wiring throughout the body, making the whole body the instrument of learning" (18). Movement creates sensory experience, which builds neural networks.

Increasingly, studies are showing the impact on learning that movement and embodied learning can have. Using movement as a way to physicalize curricular content has been linked to motivation (Fife 2003), improved science learning outcomes (Kreiser and Hairston 2007; Corbitt and Carpenter 2006; Plummer 2008), and improved math outcomes (Nemirovsky and Rasmussen 2005; Beaudoin and Johnston 2011).

Kinesthetic Learning

All of us are familiar with students who have a hard time sitting still—who learn best by moving and actually doing. These students are kinesthetic learners. Their primary mode of learning is through physical exploration and expression. Gardner, in his book *Frames of Mind* (1983), says that students who are strong kinesthetic learners have "the ability to use one's body in highly differentiated and skilled ways, for expressive as well as goal-directed purposes" (206).

In the Classroom

Celeste Miller, a teaching artist, choreographer, co-founder of Jacob's Pillow Curriculum in Motion®, and Lesley University adjunct faculty member, tells the story of one student in a kindergarten class that was learning about constellations: "The teacher had the kids sitting in a circle and she asked them to close their eyes. They sat there, faces scrunched, imagining. The teacher asked the students to visualize their favorite constellation. And students were working hard on this. Matthew begins to move around. The teacher asks him to come sit by her. Then she says to the group 'see the points of the constellation' in their mind's eye. And Matthew keeps getting up and placing his body in these different configurations. The class was videotaped. When the teacher watches the videotape later she realizes that Matthew wasn't squirming. He was forming the constellations with his body."

Often students like Matthew struggle in the traditional classroom setting, where the primary instructional method involves passive sitting and listening. This traditional mode focuses on linguistic thinking, and doesn't address students who learn better through visual, spatial, pattern, or conceptual thinking. Kinesthetic students make sense of the world through a series of complex nonlinguistic thinking functions. If we teach only to those who are strong in linguistic intelligence, we are not meeting the needs of all learners. In fact, all students can learn from engaging their bodies in learning. In order to truly meet the needs of all of our diverse learners, we must incorporate varied approaches in our teaching, including the ability to explore ideas through movement.

Education, for the most part, is designed to support linguistic approaches to learning. Not everyone processes information in the same way. The body has knowledge of its own. Ever play the piano and realize that you forgot the song, but your fingers can remember how to play? Physical memory is an important facet of learning. Researchers have found that learners acquire and store knowledge in two primary ways: *linguistic* (by reading or hearing lectures), and *nonlinguistic* (through visual imagery, kinesthetic or whole-body modes, and so forth). The more students use both systems of representing knowledge, the better they are able to think about and recall what they have learned (Marzano, Pickering, and Pollock 2001). "Not only does the body gather sensory information from the environment and send it to the brain, but it is also a site of knowledge construction and transmission" (Brownfeld 2010, 7).

Creative Movement and Higher-Order Thinking Skills

We only believe those thoughts which have been conceived not in the brain but in the whole body.

—W. B. Yeats

The processes triggered by working with the brain and body in conjunction deepen cognitive development in the categories that the new Bloom's Taxonomy (Anderson 2012) identifies as significant: creating, evaluating, analyzing, applying, understanding, remembering. This is what the Root-Bernsteins (1999) term "body thinking." The idea is that embodying ideas is a way of thinking. Don't we want to give our students as many ways as we can to construct meaning and express ideas?

Integrating movement across the curriculum works the conceptual abilities of students, which is one area of higher-order thinking where students often struggle. Students work with curricular content as raw material and physically express their understanding and knowledge of the content in their own creative movement (Miller and Glover 2010). In the creative process of making a movement representation of the concepts, students are engaging higher-order thinking skills. They are also editing and refining as they go along. They are practicing divergent thinking as they try out several ideas in order to choose the one that best expresses the concept. And they are working collaboratively.

In the Classroom

Miller and Glover (2010) give an example of a student working on an exploration of *All Quiet on the Western Front* (Remarque 1929). One student was walking to portray a soldier. "We used walk because soldiers walk! Soldiers don't twirl!" (referring to another group who had used "twirling" as their enter/exit movement choice). The artist pushed students' thinking beyond making literal connections, noting, "in a literal interpretation of the text, you will find no twirling soldiers in the book. However, a soldier's thoughts might twirl. Their heart might twirl. Perhaps their world twirls. The changing landscape might appear to twirl. And so on. This is how we can encourage our students into the realm of abstract and metaphorical thinking." The artist then shifted instructions to spark ideas in a new direction by noting, "In our work we won't be 'soldiers' but we will perhaps be their thoughts, their moods, their hopes or fears. As you make your movement choices, think about how the protagonist's thoughts move—are they heavy, burdened, spinning, recoiling? What is the change in the 'verbs' of how his thoughts can be described as moving?" Miller notes, "In creative movement we can look to movement as a way to get to thematic, conceptual, metaphoric, and symbolic analysis of the text."

Creative movement provides a unique opportunity to develop abstract thinking capacity, to think conceptually and critically. Minton suggests that "concepts can be translated into movement by producing an abstraction of the original concept" (37). By this she means that the "essence of an idea can suggest or hint at the real thing, rather than looking like the real thing" (Meecham and Sheldon cited in Minton 2003).

Abstract Thinking Through Movement

Integrating creative movement into your curriculum is an opportunity to examine particular qualities, themes, patterns, and ideas rather than telling a story as you might in drama. For example, in a second grade classroom we might ask students to show something that is solid with their bodies. Students are asked to brainstorm words as they explore ideas through shape and movement. How might you show liquid with your body? As students describe the words that come to mind as they embody the ideas of solids and liquids, you can note the emerging list of descriptors—splatter, splash, flow, trickle, stream, puddle. Find the movement quality for each and consider the differences. What's the difference between a trickle as opposed to rushing? Students translate these ideas back and forth between movement and words. You could provide some gentle coaching to guide students and encourage exploration in movement. For example, "Imagine you are a quick-moving stream…show me in your body, how the water flows, its jumps, its curves…." Students are using those great critical thinking skills. They're asked to come up with movement, and they want to make the movement qualities rich, while they're expanding an entire list of descriptive words that capture the qualities of water. Suddenly they are choreographers creating movement phrases that capture the qualities of the liquid (Celeste Miller, pers. comm.).

The ideas are actively constructed; it's experiential, and it's reflective, evolving, collaborative, and problem solving. You can ask students to use movement to find the essence of the ideas they are exploring. There are endless ways to put together movement in effort, space, and time. Students can layer in story, memory, and literal things as well as more abstract ideas. The elements of movement provide a huge palette that is at students' fingertips as they physicalize ideas. There are so many aspects of movement to explore and experiment with—ideas such as repetition, exaggeration, tempo, and order. Students use their bodies to express and explore. They make choices about how they move in space and time to express ideas. By bringing movement into the classroom, we are expanding the repertoire for learning, for assessment, and for sharing knowledge and understanding (Celeste Miller, pers. comm.).

In the Classroom

Keri Cook, a fourth grade teacher in Georgia, describes watching how students moved easily into the concept of seasons through creative movement. She says: "As I watched them craft their seasons (through creative movement activity), they needed very little input from me. It was what came natural to them. I watched them spin, and turn, and tilt, and revolve, and become unified. There was not a second of boy/girl cooties at any point. They weren't boys and girls...they were the sun, they were the earth, they were the wind, they were leaves on trees, swimming pool covers, snowmen...they were fantastic.... And they were moving...and they got it! No book, no paper, just them and their bodies."

Creative movement works as metaphor. Lakoff and Johnson (2003) describe metaphors as containers for meaning. They talk of metaphor in terms of linguistic expression, but in fact, movement creates visual and embodied metaphors. Metaphors not only make our thoughts more vivid and interesting but they actually structure our perceptions and understanding. Metaphor is exploring one idea through the frame of another. Working through movement allows us to journey into the content and explore it in new ways. "As students learn the creative movement elements of body, energy, space, and time, they also learn how to analyze and categorize their thinking" (Cornett 2003, 293).

Divergent Thinking

Ken Robinson (2006), in his TED Talk *Ken Robinson Says Schools Kill Creativity*, makes the case for needing a learning revolution to change the paradigm on traditional forms of teaching. He notes that most learning is from the head up. This is a loss. He says, "I think math is very important but so is dance. Children dance all the time if they're allowed to, we all do…. Truthfully what happens is, as children grow up we start to educate them progressively from the waist up. And then we focus on their heads. And slightly to one side."

We want our students to have creative capacity. Divergent thinking is a necessary skill for this kind of approach. Robinson (2010) defines divergent thinking as being able to identify lots of possible answers to a question—to move beyond thinking in linear ways or convergently. By engaging in an aesthetic experience through the arts, Robinson says your senses are operating at their peak. He notes a study that shows how children are naturally divergent thinkers, scoring at genius level in kindergarten, and how they lose this ability as they get older. Interestingly enough, creativity is lost as they become "educated." Robinson advocates for education that is less about conformity and more about allowing students to develop their unique talents and creativity. Can we imagine education differently by broadening our repertoire of teaching strategies in order to meet the needs of all students and support their connection to and engagement with the curriculum?

For some students, this way of knowing is critical. When students reflect on moments where movement connects them to their ideas, the case for movement in the classroom becomes compelling. "Dance allowed me to express myself without talking," and "I've always been better at nonverbal communication" (Jacobs' Pillow Dance Festival video 2010). Where would these students have been without access to movement? When information is translated into new forms such as dance, students draw upon their prior knowledge and experiences, and unique interpretations are the result. Brownfeld discusses the connection between mind and body and, drawing from John Bulwer's research, notes that in some cases, "the body can make discoveries the mind cannot" (John Bulwer cited in Brownfeld 2010, 24).

Common Core

Movement in the Common Core State Standards

Creative movement helps students develop higher-order thinking skills by translating text and speech to the symbolic language of movement and back again. As they respond to text through movement, students can make logical inferences, determine central ideas or themes, analyze how events and ideas develop over the course of a text, interpret words and phrases, and integrate and evaluate content, all of which are included in the Anchor Standards for Reading.

Getting Started With Creative Movement

In order to problem solve through dance, the most effective way to do that is to not first think but to first do. And so this requires a great deal of being able to listen to oneself, to trust oneself, and to take and intuit even when you don't really understand what you're doing. You need to first begin moving your body and allow your body to come up with some ideas. You have to go back to the mental to sort out, to edit yourself, to select out of those initial ideas what has the strongest connection, resonance with you, but first you've just got to jump in there and do something.

—Jack Bartholemew, physics teacher, 2010

Warm-Ups

Using movement as a way to warm up the body and mind can provide the immense benefits of increased oxygen flow, blood circulation, and glucose production (Jensen 2001). Movement warm-ups can be used to get the class focused, as a break to get back on task, or for a transition into a new topic. As the student physicalizes an idea, the brain forms new ways to make associations with the material being presented, creating stronger neural pathways (Zull 2002). Warm-ups, such as asking students to move in different ways, using movements that are sharp, curvy, straight, choppy, etc., and noticing how movement qualities communicate differently, are key to building skills and to using movement in a safe, constructive, community-supportive, peer-supportive way before we even go there at all.

Elements of Dance

Creative movement is a form of dance and as such utilizes the elements universal to all dance, including body, energy, space, and time (B.E.S.T.). In creative movement, understanding the basic elements of dance and the vocabulary of movement provides a place to begin looking at or "reading" movement and dance. Dance is an abstract art form, and rather than telling a story, it can reveal patterns, spatial designs, conceptual ideas, and emotions. Creative movement can add depth to the ways students investigate and know, and how they express and explore meaning. When students are provided with basic vocabulary, they can describe what they notice and how they make their choices in developing work. Share the B.E.S.T. system with students so they can access this important vocabulary.

- **B—Body** is the instrument of dance. A variety of shapes and moves can be created using the body. Movement can be done with the body as a whole unit or with isolated parts (hips, legs, feet, hands).

- **E—Energy** (or effort) is the choice of *how* to move the body. A walk sped up becomes a run. A casual walk changes when knees are lifted high, with more force, and it turns into a march. Arms can curve soft circles through the space or move sharply to resemble the motion of a robot. Emotions can be suggested depending on how a movement is performed. A run can suggest freedom or fear depending on how the energy is used and directed during the run.

- **S—Space** is where movement takes place and where it moves to and from. It can be explored by making the body big or small, or moving on different levels. Movement can travel through space in different directions (forward, backward, sideways, diagonal) and use different pathways (straight, curved, circular, zig-zag). Movements that travel through space are called *locomotor*. Examples of common locomotor movements are walking, skipping, running, and galloping. Movements done while rooted to one spot are called *axial* (think of the earth spinning on its axis). Examples of axial movements are twisting, bending, and reaching.

- **T—Time** addresses how long a movement lasts and how it is measured. Movement can be measured by counts, flavored with rhythm, or even timed to an internal, intuitive sense of how long something lasts without counts or beats. Movement can be slowed down or sped up. Movement can explore acceleration and deceleration as well as a variety of rhythms.

Every movement choice students make and execute utilizes the elements of dance. Paying attention to the elements makes movement choices and observations richer. For example, the sentence *The girl ran* can be much more interesting using the elements of dance: *The little girl lifted her knees high and threw her head back as she bounded quickly across the room to greet her father.*

Overcoming Discomfort

Understanding our own discomfort in trying something new is part of the learning curve for incorporating new teaching strategies. It takes courage to try out new ways of teaching. It will require courage on the part of the teacher and the students to try new ways of learning. A sedentary class will have a mixed response when movement is added. Some students will be joyous, others will be nervous. The nervousness caused by the newness might cause resistance and other symptoms of discomfort. We have to face our own discomfort as well—our discomfort with moving, our discomfort moving with others, our discomfort trying something new. There are societal pressures as well. At the high school level, students worry about their "coolness" and how they will be seen (Miller and Glover 2010, 7). Still, the benefits far exceed the sense of discomfort that comes with taking risks.

Introductory Activity: Movement Scores

Celeste Miller proposes a scaffolding process for using creative movement that can be broken down into four steps. This process can be accomplished in a 20–60 minute learning block depending on your classroom situation, and will engage your students in using creative movement as a tool for learning. The process begins by brainstorming about the unit of study to generate a list of descriptive and action words that will become the source for the students' movements. Then, students work in small groups to create *movement scores*, or short movement phrases that express the curricular ideas. This is followed by reflection and assessment.

1. **Brainstorm:** Brainstorm with students on a curricular topic, searching for movement words and ideas. Develop a vocabulary word and phrase list from the brainstorm and display it in the classroom. This list can be used to increase student vocabulary in general, deepen curriculum topic knowledge, and serve as a source for the students' movement-making choices.

2. **Develop movement scores:** Have students work in small groups to build their movement scores. Tell students to choose words and phrases from the brainstormed list, then select and arrange physical movements into a movement score that expresses those ideas. Introduce students to the elements of dance—body, energy, space, and time (B.E.S.T.)—with a brief introduction, a chart, or an illustration. Tell students to use B.E.S.T. to enhance their movement choices.

3. **Share:** Have students share their movement scores with their classmates. Ask the audience to use observational comments to talk both about the creative movement choices and the content connections. Ask questions to draw out learning moments in both what viewers notice and what each group learned as they developed their work.

4. **Assess:** Have students discuss or write about the process of creating movement scores, focusing on how their knowledge of curricular content changed. Create a rating scale or rubric to formally assess both the curricular content and the movement skills shown in students' movement scores.

Creative Movement Across the Curriculum

Creative movement, working with B.E.S.T., can "convey an idea, message, or emotion just as a writer would use written language to combine words and sentences into an essay or other composition" (Brownfeld 2010, 25). Engaging in the creation of creative movement work and dance as well as "viewing dance are ways to transmit nonverbal knowledge" (25). Moving between written and verbal language and nonverbal language can support the development of each. Brownfeld notes, "Where one language falls short, the other can compensate" (26). She goes on to say, "A body's actions have the ability to communicate at the same level as words...however at times the body's ability to transmit messages can surpass that of words" (28). In short, developing both verbal and nonverbal languages can strengthen communication. In the examples that follow, you will see how education can be strengthened by using "active, or embodied learning as opposed to passive learning methods, such as drilling and memorization" (38).

Creative Movement in Language Arts

When students translate text into movement, they are drawing on higher-level thinking skills. Use creative movement as a way to explore literary terms and plot lines, including exposition, setting, characters, rising action/complications, climax, falling action, and resolution/denouement from different stories. Working together in small groups, have students create a movement score (a plan for a movement phrase) exploring the use of levels and movement across space to represent their understanding. Then have students perform their pieces to show what they have learned. Incorporate creative movement into vocabulary work by having students create movements inspired by new words.

In the Classroom

A high school class read *The Maltese Falcon* (Hammet 1992) and students were asked to identify the various, often conflicting, personality traits of the main character, Sam Spade. In small groups, students selected one character trait—corrupt, ethical, amorous, or existential for example—and with paper and markers, drew a visual map of the trait's development over the course of the novel. The following steps became the means for the teacher to evoke deeply meaningful discussions, as well as finely articulated written assignments from the students about the novel's complexities.

Classroom teacher Mike Mooney worked with choreographer and Jacob's Pillow Curriculum in Motion® artist educator Nicole Livieratos and students to investigate the visual character maps as reflections of the written tone and imagery in the story. Students were asked, "How might you represent what is happening physically?" They responded by translating their maps into set spatial pathways. Next they found a section of Hammett's text that described the character trait they were working with and used it as inspiration to create movements that traveled along the spatial pathway.

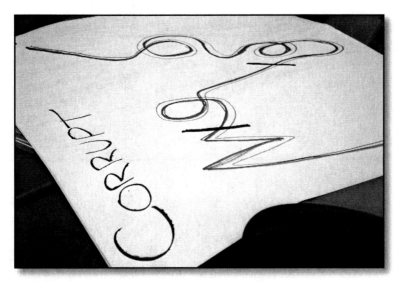

Students created visual representations of Sam Spade's path of corruption, which they represented through movement.

Mooney and Livieratos routinely shifted student attention from working on their movement studies to pausing for a discussion about the process. This enabled students to deeply tap into the gestures, behavioral patterns, energy, images, and movement styles of archetypes found in the novel, which further enhanced their movement studies. As a result, students connected to their inner feelings and experiences to create a traveling movement phrase full of rich variations in timing, rhythm, pacing, levels of the body in space, dynamics, tension, suspense, and surprising twists. Whether crawling, rolling, twirling, folding, or furling, the entire class was able to witness how character traits give shape and definition to actions and decisions made along the pathway of a novel, or one's life.

High school students presenting their movement score documenting the character pathways of Sam Spade (Jacob's Pillow Curriculum in Motion® residency).

Creative Movement in Social Studies

Use movement to explore the personal experience of people throughout history; for example, have students embody the emotions of being a slave on the Underground Railroad. Ask students to create a word or phrase with symbolic movement to show particular aspects of a time period, such as the Civil War. Students could create short creative movement pieces about the forces at work during World War II, or the range of emotions triggered by a government policy. "A dance of anger can be explosive…it can be passive anger twisting in on itself and being still and quiet" (Priscilla Harmel, pers. comm.).

Have students use movement to represent processes, such as how an ear of corn makes its way from a farmer's field to a bowl of cornflakes (Peggy Barnes, pers. comm.) or how mail makes its way from one address to another. Have them create a flow chart and bring the process to life through movement.

When working with creative movement, ask students questions such as, "What makes it less literal; what are more abstract ways to convey an idea? What happens if you make it much bigger, or much smaller? How might you play with transitions? How can you use this particular art form to express line and shape?" (Priscilla Harmel, pers. comm.)

Creative Movement in Mathematics

Ask younger students to develop choreographed movement phrases that include number patterns (e.g., 3 rows of dancers performing 4 spins each = 12 spins). Then have students share their movement pieces with classmates who identify the patterns being presented (Griss 1998). Ask students to embody geometric shapes. This can be done using their bodies or using giant elastic bands to stretch into a variety of shapes showing dimensionality. Students can create and describe patterns visually and through gesture. Have students enact mathematical problems physically, such as: *Eight birds are sitting on a telephone wire—three fly away. How many birds are left on the wire?* (Priscilla Harmel, pers. comm.).

With older students, have them demonstrate solving one- and two-step equations using creative movement, making connections between mathematical ideas and symbols. Begin with equations reflecting two expressions equal to each other. To keep the equations balanced, whatever students do on one side of the equal sign, they must also do on the other side.

Creative Movement in Science

Physicalizing scientific concepts and processes helps students internalize and truly understand. Have students show through movement the shifting of the tectonic plates of the earth and the forces at work: the oozing lava, the building pressure of magma. How do different plates move in relation to each other (i.e., convergent boundaries, divergent boundaries)? How does the movement of the plates trigger earthquakes, volcanic activity, mountain building, and oceanic trench formation along these plate boundaries? Students will discover ideas and will identify questions that need to be researched as they translate ideas in texts into movement. What do these words mean? How will they convey that meaning through physicalization? (Priscilla Harmel, pers. comm.)

Students can also use movement to show ecological shifts from unique perspectives. For example, ask students to create a movement piece examining the threat of extinction of a particular species of fish, in which they imagine the struggle of the fish. By embodying it, they come to understand in a different way.

Use movement to explore processes of many kinds. Have students work through the water cycle by first moving through the vocabulary and then embodying each phase of the cycle in movement. Ask them to imagine the force of the rain falling to the earth. How might they represent the flow of the rain coming down through their bodies? As the water dries up and evaporates it would be a different, lighter kind of movement. Students must think about how their movement can use different qualities to portray the change in the water as it moves through the cycle. There are many scientific processes that lend themselves to this kind of physical embodiment (Priscilla Harmel, pers. comm.).

Creative movement is well suited to showing action of any kind. Ask students to show in movement the timing of a particular process, how quickly a chemical reaction might move, or how sound moves through different materials. In order to create a movement piece, students will need to research what the qualities are that they want to convey and make them visible through movement (Priscilla Harmel, pers. comm.).

In the Classroom

A third grade class at the Silvio O. Conte Community School in Pittsfield, Massachusetts, culminated a Jacob's Pillow Curriculum in Motion® residency by demonstrating to the second grade what they learned about states of matter. First, the students showed solid, liquid, and gaseous states in their bodies by using moments of stillness, moving through space fluidly, and embodying the frenetic activity of molecules heated into steam. Next, the students brought these movement ideas together and physically expressed how solid transforms to liquid (melting), how liquid changes to gas (evaporation), how gas becomes liquid (condensation), and how liquid turns to solid (freezing). The creative ways in which students chose to transition between states of matter formed a captivating, artistically shaped movement phrase, and at the same time, revealed how clearly the students understood the scientific processes taking place at the molecular level behind the vocabulary (Jacob's Pillow Curriculum in Motion® 2012).

Rita Walden's second grade class in Aiken, South Carolina, created a "butterfly dance" where they moved through the phases of transformation from caterpillar to butterfly.

From caterpillar eggs, to chrysalis…

…to emerging butterfly, to flight.

Note how much is conveyed by shape and movement about what students understand about the development process. Considering the results of her arts-integrated work with students, Rita reflected, "These lessons were fun, hands-on, interesting, fact-filled ways to learn more about the butterfly. I found my students to be excited to take risks without worrying about failing…. They found their unique way of applying the knowledge they had to the activities…. I firmly believe that the hands-on approach using the arts allows a passion to come alive in students."

Assessment

You can see what students have learned by the way they translate ideas into physical form. For informal, on-the-spot assessment, ask students to answer you in movement; tell them, "Show me with your body." If you are teaching about different sources of energy, ask students to show you what happens if something is heated or cooled, or if you are working on statistics, ask students to show you their understanding of *mean, median, mode,* and *outlier*. Sometimes students who have difficulty expressing their understanding verbally or in written form will surprise you with what they know. Identifying what students have learned through movement can then provide a sense of next steps for sharing that knowledge in text-based ways as well.

In the Classroom

One teacher who tried movement in the classroom for the first time pointed out one little boy and said, "You know, I've had so much trouble with him all year because I'm not sure he's getting it. And there's a bit of a language barrier. But I watched him and every time he was asked to show his understanding in movement, I could see how deeply he understands this material because he had so many answers for me in movement."

When engaging students in more formal creative movement activities, inform them of both the curricular content and the movement principles (B.E.S.T.) they will be responsible for showing in their work. Provide students with a written list, which could be included in a simple checklist to a detailed rubric. Students should refer to these expectations when creating their movement pieces.

As students perform for the class, ask viewers (both students and teacher) to identify choreographic ideas: clear beginnings and endings, moments of surprise, variation in the work, and use of B.E.S.T. principles. Ask students, "What did you notice? What did you discover?" Viewers should describe how they saw the curricular content being expressed in the work. It is important to have students perform more than once, incorporating what they have learned from viewer feedback into new iterations of their movement pieces.

Once the final movement work has been performed, invite students to talk about their thought processes and choices as they created their work. Depending on how students unpack their thought processes, you can find out how well they understand the curriculum material, how they are using the vocabulary, and how movement supported the exploration of ideas.

Use the original checklist or rubric, along with a note-taking tool such as the one in Figure 6.1, to record your assessment of student learning. Videotaping creative movement performances and student discussion of their work will allow you to get a general sense of student understanding during the live presentation and then review the videotape later for more thorough assessment.

Figure 6.1 Note-Taking Tool for Creative Movement

How was curricular content evident in the creative movement?	
How did students utilize B.E.S.T. principles?	
How did students' discussion and explanation of their process reveal curricular understanding?	

Concluding Thoughts

Figuring out things in your body and through movement weaves ideas together. This builds a sense of intuitive knowledge, of working with an interchange of acting and responding, of physical problem solving.

—Paula Aarons

Paula Aarons, former classroom teacher and Jacobs Pillow Curriculum in Motion® artist educator notes that "when we ask students to begin moving, we find heart rate going up, changes in breathing patterns, tactile senses begin to come alive, physical senses start to operate on a higher frequency.... These are real physiological things that happen." She notes that integrating creative movement provides new pathways for learning. This physical problem solving allows students to "do first and think later as a way to generate ideas, explore concepts in new ways, draw out knowledge, and analyze through a sensory approach" (Aarons, pers. comm.). As a result, ideas are solidified and descriptive language is developed side-by-side with the movement exploration.

Aarons adds, "As educators we must remember that knowledge is not contained just in words. Intuitive knowledge matters—there is a value of experiencing feeling and feelings in the body. The content we explore in classrooms is often rational, definable, and tangible. But intuition, a felt sense of things, has an important place in learning as well" (Aarons, pers. comm.).

As Nancy King writes in her book *Giving Form to Feeling* (1975), dance (creative movement) "is surely a most extraordinary fusion of thinking, doing, and feeling. If we are concerned about the health of a child's mind, body, and spirit, then how can we ignore the education force of an art form which addresses all three at once?" We want students to become active learners. "What better way to engage them in mastering curriculum than allowing them to physically embody big ideas and nuanced knowledge through their bodies?" (Miller and Glover 2010)

Reflection

1. Thinking about your current curriculum, what opportunities do you see where movement can play a role in exploring abstract ideas or concepts?

2. What will diverse learners gain by "doing first and thinking later"?

3. How does physical problem solving occur in creative movement?

Chapter 7

Planning and Assessment

A New Lens for Planning and Assessment

To plan a unit of instruction, teachers usually begin with goals and standards, then select strategies and create activities that will lead students to those goals. In planning a unit of arts-integrated instruction, there is a third element that is an integral part of the planning process: assessment. Planning with assessment in mind ensures that a full picture of student learning emerges throughout the learning process. Formative assessment through documentation and assessment tools helps both student and teacher see where they have been and where they are going and allows them to adjust their teaching and learning processes to best achieve the stated goals. Summative assessment provides a complete picture of not only what students know, but also how they came to know and understand curricular content.

Literally translated, *assessment* means, "to sit beside." This invites the idea of a dialogue about learning that happens between teacher and student. Burnaford, Aprill, and Weiss (2001) equate assessment with research, drawing from the idea that "re/search—[meaning] to look again [is]…a process of inquiry, questioning, and looking for something" (90). Seen in this light, assessment becomes a collaborative inquiry between teacher and student investigating the teaching and learning process. Looking at arts-based processes and products can provide rich details that reveal not just *that* students know, but *how* they know.

In this chapter, we explore strategies for making assessment a core aspect of the teaching and learning process, identifying questions to explore about the learning process with students, collecting a variety of learning evidence, analyzing what the data tells us, and thinking carefully about how to tell the story of learning. Assessment drives planning and instruction in a feedback loop that moves students forward in the learning process.

Using the example of a drama-integrated social studies unit on the Oregon Trail (see the full unit plan in Appendix A), this chapter will illustrate each step of planning and implementing an integrated arts unit. The Oregon Trail Unit Planning Chart in Appendix B shows the unit goals and standards, the strategies and activities, the assessment tools that will be used, and the evidence and documentation that will be collected. In Appendix C, a blank unit planning chart is provided for your use.

Unit Planning: Capture All Three Strands

There are three strands of learning that weave together to create an arts integrated unit:

- Strand A: Content area curriculum (e.g., cellular mitosis or the Revolutionary War)

- Strand B: Arts curriculum (e.g., watercolor painting or tableaux)

- Strand C: Higher-order thinking skills

The metaphor of a braid shows the complexities of this work. Imagine the strands of evidence weaving together—each has its own content and depth, but as the strands weave, the story of learning comes together in new ways. All three strands are integral to learning, but the weaving can develop in different ways as one strand comes forward and another recedes.

In planning an arts-integrated unit, begin by identifying learning goals, standards, and curricular content. Next, plan arts strategies and activities that will help students achieve the content learning goals. Then, identify arts goals and standards that will be addressed through these integrated arts activities. Finally, analyze the activities and strategies to identify ways in which students will use higher-order thinking skills.

In the Oregon Trail unit, history and social studies standards were identified, and then three activities (improvisational role-play, tableaux, and letter writing) were created in which students could move toward meeting curriculum goals. For the drama strategies (role-play and tableaux), drama standards were selected. Finally, higher-order thinking skills were identified. The chart in Figure 7.1 shows the content, arts goals and standards, student activities, and higher-order thinking skills. See the Oregon Trail Unit Outline in Appendix A and the Oregon Trail Unit Planning Chart in Appendix B for more details.

Figure 7.1 Planning for Oregon Trail Unit

Goals and Standards	Strategy or Activity
Strand A: Content Area Goals and Standards **McREL Social Studies Standards** • Understands patterns of change and continuity in the historical succession of related events (Historical Understanding, Grade 6–8, Benchmark 4) • Understands the impact of territorial expansion on Native American tribes (United States History, Standard 9, Grade 5–6, Benchmark 4) • Understands the origins of Manifest Destiny and its influence on the westward expansion of the United States (United States History, Standard 9, Grade 5–6, Benchmark 5) **Curricular concepts:** • difficult choices facing potential settlers • hardships settlers faced in their travels • how the government prompted the Westward Movement • multiple perspectives on the Westward Movement	• Improvisational role-play • Journey tableaux • Discussion and debrief • Letters from the Trail
Strand B: Arts Goals and Standards **National Drama Standards** **Content Standard 2:** Acting by assuming roles and interacting in improvisations **Content Standard 4:** Directing by planning classroom dramatizations **Content Standard 7:** Analyzing and explaining personal preferences and constructing meanings from classroom dramatizations and from theatre	• Improvisational role-play • Journey tableaux • Discussion and debrief

Goals and Standards	Strategy or Activity
Strand C: Higher-Order Thinking Skills • **Analyze** and **apply** knowledge of the Westward Movement to a character's thoughts and actions in improvisational role-play and in letter writing • **Synthesize** information and ideas about the journey westward to **create** tableaux and write letters from the trail • **Evaluate** the effectiveness of their own and other students' role-play and tableaux in showing curricular content	• Improvisational role-play • Journey tableaux • Discussion and debrief • Letters from the Trail

Documentation: Plan to Gather Evidence

Once curricular goals, standards, arts-integrated activities, and strategies have been selected, plan how to document the process of learning. Documentation provides students with information about their progress toward meeting learning goals (formative assessment) and provides a clear picture at the end of the learning process of what students have attained (summative assessment). There are opportunities for assessing learning through students' artistic work. Collecting the right evidence reveals not just that students know, but how they know, because documentation provides a wider frame than traditional assessment. Often, work takes place in a learning situation, but is not documented well or ends up being considered a display at the end of the learning process. Documentation provides a critical feedback loop that links the objectives students set out to meet and the outcomes at which they arrive. At the beginning of a unit, plan how to document the work well through the teaching and learning process to ensure that there is evidence from which to draw in, showing that students have met the unit learning goals.

Plan to collect certain types of documentation with the objectives in mind, but as additional, unexpected learning is revealed through the arts, document evidence of that learning as well. In arts-based work, teachers never can predict every result and are more often than not happily surprised at the ideas that come forward from their students' investigations. These in-process moments help to show connections students make along the way.

Collect documentation in individual student portfolios that are available for both student and teacher to access at any time. If you are ready with a camera and a sticky note pad during student work time, you will find it easy to take quick photos or jot observations on sticky notes and place them in student portfolios at the end of the day. Also, get students in the habit of placing work samples and other evidence of learning in their portfolios. They will often surprise you with their insights into their own learning processes.

Documentation and evidence of student learning can include:

- student work samples (sketches, notes, scripts, images, storyboards, etc.)

- photos or video of student work processes

- transcripts or video of discussions and debriefings

- student journals or learning logs

- teacher observation notes

- interviews (audio or transcript)

- exit slips

- written peer or self-critiques

- assessment tools: checklists, rating scales, rubrics, and note-taking tools

Documentation in Formative Assessment

Assessment should be situated at the juncture between teaching and learning, becoming a central part of the learning process. As the researchers at Project Zero, an educational research group at Harvard University, note, "Assessment does not have to be a post-mortem. In the United States, when we think about documentation, we typically have more of a record-keeping than a learning mentality" (Project Zero 2006). Formative assessment is defined by Black and Jones (2006) as providing "information to be used as feedback, by teachers, and by their pupils in assessing themselves and each other, to modify the teaching and learning activities in which they are engaged" throughout the process of learning. This means that formative assessment strategies are ongoing throughout the process of learning, providing teachers with information about where they need to go next with their teaching, and providing students with ongoing feedback.

In arts-integrated learning, this means looking at what is discovered in the creative process as students discuss their creative choices and reflect on how they have translated ideas into new forms. Thinking together throughout the learning journey allows both student and teacher to course correct as needed. As teachers see how students are accessing content and expressing their understanding, they can adjust their teaching to provide the right next step for students as they learn. Larry Ferlazzo (2012) notes, "When students are asked to think about what they have learned and how they have learned it (the learning strategies they've used), they are better able to understand their own learning processes and can set new goals for themselves."

This back and forth progression is made easier with documentation to draw from. As students show their work through sketches, notes, scripts, video, images, audiotapes, and other documentation, and share ideas through discussions and debriefing, learning logs and journals, and conferencing, they can self-assess, work with peers for feedback, and conference with the teacher for a clear picture of where they are in achieving objectives and what they need to do next to deepen their learning.

In the Oregon Trail unit, formative assessment documentation includes:

- video of improvised role-play

- verbal peer feedback and student self-critique while viewing video of role-play, documented in teacher notes

- role-play note-taking tool completed by teacher

- storyboards, notes, and other artifacts used by students in creation of tableaux

- photographs of in-process tableaux

- rating scale completed by actors, peers, and teacher critiquing in-process tableaux slide shows

Documentation in Summative Assessment

Summative assessment evaluates what has been learned at the end of the process. In addition to traditional paper-and-pencil testing, look at the entire learning process through the documentation that has been collected in student portfolios. Arter and Spandel (1991) describe the portfolio as "a purposeful collection of student work that tells the story of the student's efforts, progress, or achievement in (a) given area(s). This collection must include student participation in selection of portfolio content, the guidelines for selection, the criteria for judging merit, and evidence of student self-reflection."

Portfolios allow teachers to do the following:

- collaborate with students to document a more detailed picture of student learning

- include evidence of learning that occurs throughout the creative process, not just a cumulative product at the end

- track how students arrive at an answer (this can be as important as the answer itself)

- use authentic approaches to work that mirror real-life contexts.

Students should be equal partners in the process of creating and reflecting on the work collected to tell the story of their learning. Students can be at the center of telling their own stories, helping to document processes, select work samples, collect reflections, and organize materials in a thoughtful way that communicates well.

Portfolios can be used to review progress with students and parents. Looking together at a wide range of evidence can lead to reflective conversations that are useful for both you and your students. Portfolios also provide evidence of how well students have achieved goals, benchmarks, and standards for grade determination.

For the Oregon Trail unit, final summative assessment, assembled in student portfolios, includes:

- teacher notes on observations made during formative assessments

- photographs of the final tableaux

- teacher and student rating scales on final tableaux

- student-written Letters from the Trail

- teacher-completed rubric for Letters from the Trail

Exhibition

Showing student work in an exhibition or public performance can provide strong summative evidence of how students work with curricular ideas as they translate content into artistic work that reveals understanding. Sharing the work with an outside audience can:

- provide opportunities for students to record their learning process

- allow for critique, which is a natural outgrowth of the process of art making and can prompt reflection and discussion both on a personal level and in peer-to-peer critique as students comment on each other's work

- give a visual documentation of students' progress

- provide time and space for review and discussion of work

Assessment Tools

In addition to documenting student work through the collection of evidence, plan to create and use note-taking tools, checklists, rating scales, and rubrics to formally evaluate how the evidence shows students' attainment of learning goals. These assessment tools should be used not only by the teacher, but also as peer feedback and student self-critique during the creative process. All these tools can be used in both formative and summative evaluation, but each tool provides a different level of detail and specificity. As part of unit planning, create assessment tools and decide when and how they will be used. Collect completed assessment tools in student portfolios as part of an overall picture of student learning.

Note-Taking Tools

The simplest assessment tool focuses observation without requiring evaluation or rating. Create a note-taking chart, such as the one shown in Figure 7.2, or a simple list of questions to guide observation of student work and provide focus on specific standards and goals. A note-taking tool completed by a teacher or peers can provide valuable formative feedback to students during the creative process, as well as describing evidence of student learning at the end of a unit of study.

Figure 7.2 Oregon Trail: Note-Taking Tool for Role-Play

	Student name:
How did the student show his/her character's feelings and thoughts?	
What curricular content was evident in the role-play?	
How did the student's explanation of his or her process reveal curricular understanding?	

Checklists

Arnold Aprill (2011), founding and creative director of Chicago Arts Partnerships in Education (CAPE), notes that checklists help teachers see "the simple presence or absence of characteristics, actions, and qualities." There is no evaluation made of the work; a checklist simply shows what is and is not present. Figure 7.3 shows a checklist used in the Oregon Trail unit.

As formative assessment, students can use checklists as a quick measure of whether or not they are on track and what they need to add to their work. Checklists can also be used as summative assessment to show that students have met the requirements of an assignment or project. Checklists can note the inclusion of both content area and arts components.

Figure 7.3 Oregon Trail Unit: Checklist of Expectations for Letters from the Trail

Students have done the following:

- ❏ shown the perspective of the character

- ❏ used source material to inform work

- ❏ depicted events that may well have occurred during the time period

- ❏ addressed choices and difficulties the character faced

- ❏ articulated emotion the character would have experienced

Rating Scales

A rating scale is used to show how students have demonstrated learning goals on a continuum. For each learning goal or assignment requirement, respondents choose a statement or number to indicate students' level of attainment of that goal or requirement. This is one step beyond a checklist, showing not only whether students have included required components, but also how well they have addressed the requirements. A rating sheet is not as thorough as a rubric, and does not take as long to complete, providing a quick way to give students feedback on their work. Figure 7.4 shows an example of a rating scale.

As formative evaluation, rating sheets tell students where they are in the process of addressing requirements and where they need to do more work. They can be used as teacher-, peer-, or self-critique. As summative evaluation, rating sheets show evaluation of completed work measured against standards and goals.

Figure 7.4 Oregon Trail Unit: Tableaux Rating Scale

Directions: Rate how effectively students have addressed each requirement on a scale from 1 to 5, 1 meaning "not at all" and 5 meaning "highly effectively."

How Effectively Have Students . . .	Rating
depicted a scene that is relevant to the study of the Oregon Trail?	1 2 3 4 5
demonstrated in their dramatic choices or in discussion evidence of the translation of ideas from the text into dramatic form?	1 2 3 4 5
created realistic representation of characters?	1 2 3 4 5
demonstrated use of source material in their dramatic work?	1 2 3 4 5
shown an understanding of opportunities afforded by the Westward Expansion?	1 2 3 4 5
shown an understanding of challenges afforded by the Westward Expansion?	1 2 3 4 5
demonstrated examples of decisions made by settlers?	1 2 3 4 5
Notes:	

Rubrics

Rubrics, like rating scales, evaluate performance characteristics on levels, indicating the degree to which a standard or requirement has been met. But, unlike the numbers on a rating scale, a rubric includes specific descriptions of each rating, telling exactly how students' work addresses learning goals.

Teacher-created rubrics should be available to students at the beginning of the learning process so they can see specifically what they are expected to do or show. Whenever possible, involve students in creating rubrics to increase investment and ownership of the process and to provide students with an opportunity to think about learning from an outcomes perspective. Learning is deepened when teachers and students collaborate on setting expectations and reviewing the evidence of learning together.

As formative assessment, rubrics provide specific, detailed descriptions for students of how their work will be measured. Use rubrics as both peer feedback and student self-critique so that students can evaluate their own work and revise as necessary. As summative assessment, rubrics show in detail how students have demonstrated their understanding and to what extent they have attained standards and learning goals. Rubrics should address both content area and arts standards and goals. The rubric in Figure 7.5 is for summative evaluation of the tableaux activity.

Figure 7.5 Oregon Trail Tableaux Rubric

Assessment Criteria	Proficient	Developing	Unsatisfactory
Analyzes and applies change and continuity of relationships to a variety of historical issues, events, and problems	Creates dramatizations that demonstrate analysis of historical moments	Creates dramatizations that depict historical moments and is beginning to articulate choices based on content	Creates scenes that do not reflect historical reality
Explains how key individuals and events influenced the Westward Expansion movement	Creates dramatic representations that show the complexity of settlers' experiences and decisions	Depicts decisions and experiences simplistically	Creates scenes that do not document specific decisions and experiences
Uses primary and secondary sources to create a believable narrative about the Westward Expansion	Uses source material to inform the development of detailed dramatizations of events and issues	Incorporates broad themes from source documents into dramatizations	Does not incorporate sources into their dramatizations
Creates detailed characters that illuminate relationships, choices, and dilemmas of historical period	Creates characters and relationships that depict the choices and challenges settlers faced	Creates characters that identify relationships choices and challenges in a basic way	Creates characters that are one dimensional with limited relationship to each other

Figure 7.5 Oregon Trail Tableaux Rubric *(cont.)*

Assessment Criteria	Proficient	Developing	Unsatisfactory
Plans a compelling and effective dramatization that draws on historical facts	Creates a drama that incorporates dramatic conflict based on historical fact	Creates a drama that though not fully developed incorporates historical fact	Dramatizations show limited planning
Analyzes and explains personal preferences and constructs meanings from classroom dramatizations	Articulates clear rationale for creation of dramatization	Able to articulate the main historical themes included in dramatizations	Not able to describe the choices made in the process of working with historical content in a drama

A Complete Picture of Learning

At the end of a unit of instruction, student portfolios provide a complete picture of student learning, showing both what they know and how they came to know it. Through documentation gathered during the learning process and completed assessment tools, a true picture emerges of each student's achievements. Share portfolios with parents and other stakeholders to provide evidence that teaching through the arts not only addresses standards, but also takes students on an in-depth journey of learning.

Concluding Thoughts

We hear increasingly about data-driven decision making. The need to collect evidence and use it to inform decisions makes sense, particularly in understanding what students have learned, how they have learned, what teaching has been effective for student learning, and where improvement is needed. Unfortunately, the data is too often drawn from a narrow focus on content knowledge and skill. The arts can provide a more layered look at students' learning. There are many aspects of learning and expression taking place in the creative process, and mindful, well-constructed documentation can make these learning strands visible and honor the complexity of teaching and learning.

Writer Natalie Goldberg (1998) notes that by writing about our experiences, "We live our life twice." In other words, we have the opportunity to reflect on and explore what has happened to us and the choices we have made, and to notice the specifics of what we have been involved with and how we have made meaning of it. This is true of the process of documentation, as well. If we engage our students in the documentation process, asking them to think about how to put together traces of learning in ways that tell the story of learning, they will learn about their own processes and how their choices affect their learning. In addition, we as teachers will gain valuable insight about our teaching choices and learning, and about what we value, as well as assessing how we have met the objectives of our curriculum.

Teachers who integrate the arts often describe the results as transformative—for them and for the way they see student learning. The arts provide flexible ways for students to represent their understanding. Taking the time to collect and share evidence of this understanding can help teachers and students reveal the layers of learning that occur in this type of work. Students who are provided artistic avenues for expressing understanding and sharing their ideas in different symbolic systems or languages can bring forward individual voice and perspective. Taken together, using all the languages available to us, this type of assessment provides a more holistic and human view of learners. We are able to tell their stories in all their complexity.

Reflection

1. What are some advantages of documenting the creative process of learning over traditional testing alone?

2. How might careful documentation expand upon the use of assessment tools?

3. What benefits do students gain by reviewing documentation alongside teachers?

Oregon Trail Unit Outline

Note: These activities should follow initial study of the Westward Expansion.

The Invitation to Travel West

Tell students that they are families in Massachusetts that have been invited to a town hall meeting where a guest from the United States government is interested in talking with them about free land out West. Speak to students (teacher in role) as a government representative offering free land and support for the journey. Discuss the opportunity for settlers and suggest they need to act now.

Family Decision Role-Play

Group students into "families" and have them role-play an improvised discussion about whether or not they should go west. Each student should self-select a family member role. Ask students to put themselves in the place of their characters, thinking about how the decision to move west would affect them individually and as families, both negatively and positively. At the end of the role-play, each family must decide whether or not to make the journey. Videotape each group's role-play.

As a class, view each role-play video. Discuss each group's performance, focusing on students' portrayals of reasons for and against taking the journey west. Take notes as students self and peer critique. Use the note-taking tool to record your observations of the role-play to evaluate what additional information and sources students need to inform their understanding of the Westward Expansion.

Journey Tableaux

Ask students to assemble in their family groups from the role-play activity. Tell students that each family will be making the journey west (regardless of the decision made during role-play). Have each group work together to create a series of three tableaux (frozen scenes) showing three moments from their journey:

- leaving home to begin the journey

- two months into the journey

- one year later

Tell students they will need to use everything they have learned about Westward Expansion to create realistic scenes and provide clear explanations of their reasoning. Provide students with a copy of the rubric that will be used to evaluate their tableaux. Tell students they can create storyboards, notes, or any other artifacts to show their thought processes.

Have students share their in-process tableaux with the class and explain their thinking, then debrief using a rating scale for teacher, self, and peer critique. Students should use the feedback they receive to improve their work.

When students are satisfied with their tableaux, hold a formal viewing presentation. Save all in-process artifacts and photograph each group's final tableaux for documentation. Complete the rubric for summative evaluation.

Letters from the Trail

Have students write letters from their characters to friends who did not make the journey west. Students should write about why they made the journey, detail significant events along the way, and share their hopes for the future. Provide students with a checklist of expectations to guide their letter writing. Students' letters will provide summative evidence of their learning for this unit.

This unit uses O'Neill and Lambert's approach detailed in their book *Drama Structures* to bring new life to textbook descriptions about the Westward Movement and the Oregon Trail (O'Neill and Lambert 1991).

Appendix B

Oregon Trail Unit Planning Chart

Goals and Standards	Strategy or Activity	Assessment Tools	Evidence/ Documentation
Strand A: Content Area Goals and Standards **McREL Social Studies Standards** • Understands patterns of change and continuity in the historical succession of related events (Historical Understanding, Grade 6-8, Benchmark 4) • Understands the impact of territorial expansion on Native American tribes (United States History, Standard 9, Grade 5-6, Benchmark 4) • Understands the origins of Manifest Destiny and its influence on the westward expansion of the United States (United States History, Standard 9, Grade 5-6, Benchmark 5) **Curricular concepts:** • difficult choices facing potential settlers • hardships settlers faced in their travels • how the government prompted the Westward Expansion • multiple perspectives on the Westward Expansion	• Improvisational role-play • Journey tableaux • Discussion and debrief • Letters from the Trail	**Formative:** • Role-play note-taking tool • Tableaux rating scale **Summative:** • Final tableaux rating scale • Letters from the Trail checklist • Tableaux rubric • Chapter test	**Formative:** • Video of improvised character role-play • Teacher notes on role-play debrief • Photographs of in-process tableaux • Students' storyboards, notes on tableaux process **Summative:** • Photographs of final tableaux • Letters from the Trail

Goals and Standards	Strategy or Activity	Assessment Tools	Evidence/ Documentation
Strand B: Arts Goals and Standards **National Drama Standards** **Content Standard 2:** Acting by assuming roles and interacting in improvisations **Content Standard 4:** Directing by planning classroom dramatizations **Content Standard 7:** Analyzing and explaining personal preferences and constructing meanings from classroom dramatizations and from theatre	• Improvisational role-play • Journey tableaux • Discussion and debrief	**Formative:** • Role-play note-taking tool • Tableaux rating scale **Summative:** • Final tableaux rating scale • Tableaux rubric	**Formative:** • Video of improvised character role-play • Teacher notes on role-play debrief • Photographs of in-process tableaux • Students' storyboards, notes on tableaux process **Summative:** • Photographs of final tableaux • Teacher notes on peer critique and discussion
Strand C: Higher-Order Thinking Skills • **Analyze** and **apply** knowledge of the Westward Expansion to a character's thoughts and actions in improvisational role-play and in letter writing • **Synthesize** information and ideas about the journey westward to **create** tableaux and write letters from the trail • **Evaluate** the effectiveness of their own and other students' role-play and tableaux in showing curricular content	• Improvisational role-play • Journey tableaux • Discussion and debrief • Letters from the Trail	**Formative:** • Role-play note-taking tool • Tableaux rating scale **Summative:** • Final tableaux rating scale • Tableaux rubric	**Formative:** • Video of improvised character role-play • Teacher notes on role-play debrief • Students' storyboards, notes on tableaux process **Summative:** • Photographs of final tableaux • Letters from the Trail • Teacher notes on peer critique and discussion

Unit Planning Chart

Goals and Standards	Strategy or Activity	Assessment Tools	Evidence/ Documentation
Strand A: Content Area Goals and Standards			
Strand B: Arts Goals and Standards			
Strand C: Higher-Order Thinking Skills			

Appendix D

Recommended Resources

Poetry Resources

Creech, Sharon. 2008. *Hate that Cat*. New York: HarperCollins Children's Books.

Dickinson, Emily. 1990. "Not in Vain." In *Emily Dickinson: Selected Poems*, 42. Edited by Stanley Appelbaum. Mineola, NY: Dover Thrift Editions.

Franco, Betsy. 2009. *Messing Around the Monkey Bars*. Somerville, MA: Candlewick.

Heaney, Seamus. 1995. "Scaffolding." In *Death of a Naturalist*. London: Faber and Faber.

———. 1999. "The Rain Stick." In *Opened Ground: Selected Poems 1966–1996*. London: Faber and Faber.

Hughes, Langston. 2007 (1932). "Dreams." In *The Dream Keeper and Other Poems*. New York: Knopf Books for Young Readers.

Katz, Alan. 2008. *Oops!* New York: Simon & Schuster Children's Publishing.

Kipling, Rudyard. 2007. "If–." In *Kipling: Poems*, 170–171. New York: Everyman's Library.

Nesbitt, Kenn. 2006. "The Aliens Have Landed." In *The Aliens Have Landed at Our School*. Minnetonka, MN: Meadowbrook Press.

Prelutsky, Jack. 1984. *New Kid on the Block*. New York: Greenwillow Books.

———. 1996. *A Pizza the Size of the Sun*. New York: Greenwillow Books.

———. 2005. *Raining Pigs and Noodles*. New York: HarperCollins.

———. 2008. "Be Glad Your Nose Is on Your Face." In *Be Glad Your Nose Is on Your Face And Other Poems: Some of the Best of Jack Prelutsky*, 152. New York: Greenwillow Books.

Shields, Carol D. 2003. *Almost Late to School*. New York: Dutton Children's Books.

Silverstein, Shel. 1974. *Where the Sidewalk Ends*. New York: HarperCollins.

———. 1981. *A Light in the Attic*. New York: HarperCollins.

———. 1996. *Falling Up*. New York: HarperCollins.

Soto, Gary. 1995. "Oranges." In *Gary Soto: New and Selected Poems*, 72–73. San Francisco, CA: Chronicle Books.

Viorst, Judith. 1982. "If I Were in Charge of the World." In *If I Were in Charge of the World and Other Worries*, 2. New York: Simon & Schuster.

Music Resources

East, Helen. 1989. *The Singing Sack: 28 Song-Stories from Around the World*. London: A and C Black.

Jones, Bessie. 1972. *Step It Down: Games, Plays, Songs and Stories From the Afro-American Heritage*. Athens, GA: The University of Georgia Press.

Pascale, Louise. 2011. *Qu Qu Qu Barg-e-Chinaar: Children's Songs from Afghanistan*. Cambridge, MA: Children's Songs from Afghanistan. http://www.afghansongbook.org/.

Putumayo. 1999. *World Playground*. Putumayo World Music, ASIN B00000JT4P, 1999, compact disc.

Sound Resources

Schafer, R. Murray. 1992. *A Sound Education: 100 Exercises in Listening and Sound-making.* Indian River, Ontario, Canada: Arcana Editions.

Instrument Making Resources

deBeer, Sara., ed. 1995. *Open Ears: Musical Adventures for a New Generation.* Roslyn, NY: Ellipsis Kids.

Langstaff, John, and Ann Sayre Wiseman. 2003. *Making Music: 70 Improvisational Musical Instruments to Make and Play.* North Adams, MA: Storey Publishing.

Sabbeth, Alex. 1997. *Rubber-Band Banjos and a Java Jive Bass: Projects and Activities on the Science of Music and Sound.* New York: John Wiley and Songs, Inc.

Videos

Benjamin Zander: The transformative power of classical music. http://www.ted.com/talks/benjamin_zander_on_music_and_passion.html.

> Benjamin Zander has two infectious passions: classical music and helping all of us realize our untapped love for it—and by extension, our untapped love for all new possibilities, new experiences, and new connections.

Bobbie McFerrin plays...the audience! http://www.ted.com/talks/bobby_mcferrin_hacks_your_brain_with_music.html.

In this fun, 3-minute performance from the World Science Festival, musician Bobby McFerrin uses the pentatonic scale to reveal one surprising result of the way our brains are wired.

Choir (Perpetuum Jazzile) create a rainstorm with hands: http://www.youtube.com/watch?v=BC8re5HvOGI.

This is a great performance by Perpetuum Jazzile using only their hands to create a sound story. You can almost smell the rain!

Eric Whitacre, Virtual Choir : http://www.ted.com/talks/lang/en/eric_whitacre_a_virtual_choir_2_000_voices_strong.html.

In a moving and madly viral video, composer Eric Whitacre leads a virtual choir of singers from around the world. The stunning part of his talk is the story behind the choir. Eric talks through the creative challenges of making music powered by YouTube, and unveils the first 2 minutes of his new work, "Sleep," with a video choir of 2,052. The full piece premiered in 2011 (yes, on YouTube!).

MOZART at the Office: http://www.youtube.com/watch?v=tYOVh2QNjHA.

Mozart is timeless, even when played on office "stuff" such as coffee cups, water glasses, coffee pots, and metal trashcans!

Stomp! http://www.youtube.com/watch?v=US7c9ASVfNc.

Rhythm and sound created in unexpected ways using everyday objects.

The Vegetable Orchestra: http://www.vegetableorchestra.org.

> Worldwide one of a kind, the Vegetable Orchestra performs on instruments made of fresh vegetables. The utilization of various, ever-refined vegetable instruments creates a musically and aesthetically unique sound universe.

Storytelling Resources

Center for Digital Storytelling: http://www.storycenter.org/.

Chase, Richard. 1976. "Soap, Soap, Soap." In *Grandfather Tales*, 115–122. New York: Houghton Mifflin Company.

Digital Story Telling: http://www.northeastern.edu/edtech/teaching_learning/teaching_tools/digital_story.

Digital Storytelling Lesson Plans. http://www.lessonplanet.com/search?keywords=digital+storytelling&media=lesson.

> This site provides teachers with many examples of digital storytelling for a wide range of grade levels, for example: the history of the American flag, grades 3–5; digital color poetry, grades 3–5; culture creation vs. culture consumption, 9th grade; integrating grammar and literature, grades 9–12.

Galdone, Paul. 1975. *The Gingerbread Boy*. New York: Houghton Mifflin Company.

Jacobs, Joseph, ed. 2007. "Lazy Jack." In *English Fairy Tales*. New York: Everyman's Library.

MacDonald, Margaret Read. 1986. "Hic Hic Hic." In *Twenty Tellable Tales*. Chicago: American Library Association.

———. 1986. "Jack and the Robbers." In *Twenty Tellable Tales*. Chicago, IL: American Library Association.

MacDonald, Margaret Read. 2000. "Little Boy Frog and Little Boy Snake." In *Shake-It-Up Tales!*, 134–139. Little Rock, AR: August House.

———. 2000. "What a Wonderful Life!" In *Shake-It-Up Tales!*, 115–124. Little Rock, AR: August House.

———. 2001. "The Lost Mitten." In *The Parent's Guide to Storytelling*, 26–33. Little Rock, AR: August House.

———. 2001. "The Wide Mouth Frog." In *The Parent's Guide to Storytelling*, 83–87. Little Rock, AR: August House.

———. 2006. *The Squeaky Door*. New York: HarperCollins Children's Books.

Morgan, Pierr. 1990. *The Turnip*. New York: Philomel.

Paye, Won-Ldy, and Margaret H. Lippert. 2002. *Head, Body, Legs*. New York: Henry Holt and Company.

Pellowski, Anne. 1984. "The Black Cat." In *The Story Vine*. New York: Aladdin.

———. 1984. *The Story Vine: A Book of Unusual and Easy-to-tell Stories From Around the World*. New York: Macmillan Publishing Company.

———. 1987. "Brothers Tall and Brothers Small." In *The Family Storytelling Handbook*. New York: Simon & Schuster Children's Publishing.

———. 1995. "The King's Diamond Cross." In *The Storytelling Handbook*. New York: Simon & Schuster Children's Publishing.

Schimmel, Nancy. 1992. "The Rain Hat." In *Just Enough to Make a Story*, 22–24. Berkeley, CA: Sisters' Choice Books and Recordings.

———. 1992. "The Tailor." In *Just Enough to Make a Story*, 2–3. Berkeley, CA: Sisters' Choice Books and Recordings.

The Educational Uses of Digital Storytelling: http://digitalstorytelling.coe.uh.edu/.

The Elements of Digital Storytelling: http://www.inms.umn.edu/elements/.

Creative Movement Resources

BrainDance. http://creativedance.org/about/braindance/.

Brain Gym®. http://www.braingym.org/.

MeMoves™. http://www.thinkingmoves.com/.

Research Resources

The Arts Education Partnership. http://www.artsedsearch.org/.

> "AEP has developed *ArtsEdSearch* as a resource for policymakers and education stakeholders and leaders to better understand and articulate the role that arts education can play in meeting" the challenge of "preparing students to succeed in the changing contexts of the 21st century."

The President's Committee on Arts and Humanities. http://www.pcah.gov/.

> "The PCAH believes that the arts and humanities should be a part of the education of every child in America and honors organizations and supports initiatives that give young people the opportunity to experience the mastery, discipline, and accomplishment that is part of being an artist and a scholar." This website lists arts and humanities research findings and publications.

Appendix E

References Cited

Adams, Gerald. R. 1985. "Identity and Political Socialization." In *Adolescence: Processes and Contents*, edited by A. S. Waterman. San Francisco, CA: Jossey-Bass Inc.

Anderson, Lorin. 2012. "Bloom's Taxonomy, New Version." Old Dominion University. Accessed June 6. http://www.odu.edu/educ/roverbau/Bloom/blooms_taxonomy.htm.

Aprill, Arnold. 2011. "What do we measure how?" Chicago Arts Partnerships in Education, Arts Assessment Toolbox. Accessed June 11. http://www.artsassessment.org/wp-content/uploads/2011/05/Assessment-Instrument-Guide.pdf.

Arter, Judy, and Vicki Spandel. 1991. *Using Portfolios of Student Work in Instruction and Assessment*. Portland, OR: Northwest Regional Educational Laboratory.

Banks, James A. 1994. *An Introduction To Multicultural Education*. Boston: Allyn and Bacon.

Beach, Richard, Deborah Appleman, Susan Hynds, and Jeffrey Wilhelm. 2002. *Teaching Literature to Adolescents*. New York: Lawrence Erlbaum Associates, Inc.

Beaudoin, Colleen, and Pattie Johnston, P. 2011. "The Impact Of Purposeful Movement In Algebra Instruction." *Education* 132 (1): 82–96.

Bellisario, Kerrie, Lisa Donovan and Monica Prendergast. 2011. "Promising Pathways: Studies on Arts Integration." Cambridge, MA: Lesley University.

Bellisario, Kerrie, and Lisa Donovan with Monica Prendergast. 2012. *Voices from the Field: Investigating Teachers' Perspectives on the Relevance of Arts Integration in Their Classrooms*. Cambridge, MA: Lesley University.

Birge, Edward Bailey. 1984. *History of Public School Music in the United States*. Boston, MA: Oliver Ditson Company.

Black, Paul, and Jane Jones. 2006. "Formative Assessment and the Learning and Teaching of MFL: Sharing the Learning Road Map with the Learners." *Language Learning Journal* 34 (1): 4–9.

Boal, Augusto. 1995. *The Rainbow of Desire: The Boal Method of Theater And Therapy*. New York: Routledge.

———. 2002. *Games for Actors and Non-Actors*. London: Routledge.

Booth, Eric. 1999. *The Everyday Work of Art: Awakening The Extraordinary in Your Daily Life*. Naperville, IL: Sourcebooks, Inc.

Bradby, Marie. 2000. *Mama, Where Are You From?* New York: Orchard Books.

Brownfeld, Jessica Marie. 2010. "The Dancing Classroom: Bringing the Body into Education Through the Creative Process." Bachelor of Arts Thesis. Middletown, CT: Wesleyan University.

Burdette, Martha. 2011. "Arts Integration: The Authentic Context for 21st Century Learning." The Southeast Center for Arts Integration. http://centerforartsintegration.org/articles/arts-integration/.

Burnaford, Gail, Arnold Aprill, and Cynthia Weiss. 2001. *Renaissance in the Classroom: Arts Integration and Meaningful Learning*. Mahwah, NJ: Lawrence Erlbaum.

Carey, Nancy, Elizabeth Farris, Michael Sikes, Rita Foy, and Judi Carpenter. 1995. "Arts in Education in Public Elementary and Secondary Schools" NCES No. 95-082. Washington, DC: U.S. Department of Education; Office of Educational Research and Improvement. ERIC, ED388607.

Carr, Margaret. 2001. *Assessment In Early Childhood Settings: Learning Stories.* Thousand Oaks, CA: Sage Publications Inc.

Christensen, Linda. 2001 "Where I'm From: Inviting Students' Lives into the Classroom." *Rethinking Schools* Winter 1997/1998: 22–23.

Common Core State Standards Initiative. 2010. *Common Core State Standards.* Washington, DC: National Governors Association Center for Best Practices and the Council of Chief State School Officers. http://www.corestandards.org/.

Conklin, Wendy. 2009. *Differentiation Strategies: Mathematics.* Huntington Beach, CA: Shell Education.

Corbitt, Cynthia, and Molly Carpenter. 2006. "The Nervous System Game." *Science and Children* 43 (6): 26–29.

Cordova, Ralph. Jr. 2008. "Writing and Painting Our Lives into Being: School, Home, And The Larger Community As Transformative Spaces For Learning." *Language Arts.* 86 (1): 18-27. ERIC, EJ807172.

Cornett, Claudia. 2003. *Creating Meaning Through Literature and the Arts: An Integration Resource for Classroom Teachers,* 2nd ed. Upper Saddle River, NJ: Pearson Education Ltd.

Deasy, Richard. 2002. *Critical Links: Learning in the Arts and Student Academic and Social Development.* Washington, DC: Arts Education Partnership.

Dewey, John. 1931. *Philosophy and Civilization.* New York: Minton.

———. 1934. *Art as Experience.* New York: Minton.

Doherty, Timothy J. 1996. "College Writing and the Resources of Theatre." Unpublished dissertation, University of Massachusetts.

Donovan, Lisa. 2005. "The Aesthetics of Listening: Creating Spaces for Learning." Doctoral dissertation, Lesley University.

Donovan, Lisa, Richard Shreefter, and Marianne Adams. 2005. *Curriculum Resource Guide: A Sharing of Arts Based Strategies for Learning.* Cambridge, MA: Creative Arts in Learning Division at Lesley University National Arts & Learning Collaborative (NALC). http://www.artslearning.org/files/NEACurriculumResourceGuide.pdf.

Dooley, Roger. July 29, 2010. "Stories Synchronize Brains." *Neuromarketing: Where Brain Science and Marketing Meet* (blog). Accessed June 11, 2012. http://www.neurosciencemarketing.com/blog/articles/stories-synchronize-brains.htm.

Dudding, Kate. 2005. "The Value of Storytelling in Education." KateDudding.com. Accessed June 11, 2012. http://www.katedudding.com/value-storytelling-education.htm.

Dunleavy, Jodene, and Penny Milton. 2008. "Student Engagement for Effective Teaching and Deep Learning." *Education Canada* 48 (5): 4–8.

Ferlazzo, Larry. "Response: Ways to Include Students in the Formative Assessment Process." *Classroom Q&A with Larry Ferlazzo*, Education Week Teacher blog. January 10, 2012. Accessed June 11, 2012. http://blogs.edweek.org/teachers/classroom_qa_with_larry_ferlazzo/2012/01/matt_townsley_asked_carol_boston.html.

Fife, Britney Michelle. 2003. "A Study of First Grade Children and Their Recall Memory When Using Active Learning in Mathematics." Masters Thesis, Johnson Bible College.

Fiske, Edward B., ed. 1999. *Champions of Change: The Impact of the Arts on Learning.* Washington, DC: Arts Education Partnership.

Frye, Elizabeth M., Woodrow Trathen, and Bob Schlagal. 2010. "Extending Acrostic Poetry into Content Learning: a Scaffolding Framework." *The Reading Teacher* 63 (7): 591–595.

Gallas, Karen. 1991. "Art As Epistemology: Enabling Children to Know What They Know." *Harvard Educational Review* 61 (1): 40–51.

Gardner, Howard E. 1983. *Frames of Mind: The Theory of Multiple Intelligences.* New York: Basic Books.

Gere, Jeff, Beth-Ann Kozlovich, and Daniel A. Kelin, II. 2002. *By Word of Mouth: A Storytelling Guide for the Classroom.* Honolulu, HI: Pacific Resources for Education and Learning.

Gill, Sharon Ruth. 2007. "The Forgotten Genre Of Children's Poetry." *The Reading Teacher* 60 (7): 622–625.

Goldberg, Merryl. 2012, *Arts Integration: Teaching Subject Matter Through the Arts in Multicultural Settings,* 4th ed. Boston, MA: Pearson Education, Inc.

Goldberg, Merryl, and Ann Phillips, eds. 1995. "Arts as Education." *Harvard Educational Review* 24.

Goldberg, Natalie. 1998. *Writing Down the Bones: Freeing the Writer Within.* Boston, MA: Shambhala.

Goral, Mary Barr, and Cindy Meyers Gnadinger. 2006. "Using Storytelling to Teach Mathematics Concepts." *Australian Primary Mathematics* 11 (1): 4–8. ERIC, EJ793906.

Gordon, John. 2009. "Sounds Right: Pupils Responses to Heard Poetry and the Revised National Curriculum for English." *The Curriculum Journal* 20 (2): 161–175.

Graves, James Bau. 2005. *Cultural Democracy: The Arts, Community and Public Purpose*. Chicago, IL: University of Illinois Press.

Greene, Maxine. 1978. *Landscapes of Learning*. New York: Teachers College Press.

————. 1992. "The Passion of Pluralism: Multiculturalism and the Expanding Community." *Journal of Negro Education* 61 (3): 250–261.

Griss, Susan. 1998. *Minds in Motion*. Portsmouth, NH: Heinemann.

Grove, Robin, Catherine Stevens, and Shirley McKechnie. 2005. *Thinking in Four Dimensions: Creativity and Cognition in Contemporary Dance*. Carlton, Victoria, Australia: Melbourne University Press.

Hamilton, Martha, and Mitch Weiss. 2005. *Children Tell Stories: Teaching and Using Storytelling in the Classroom*, 2nd ed. New York: Richard C. Owen Publishers, Inc.

Hammet, Dashiel. 1992. *The Maltese Falcon*. New York: Vintage Books.

Hannaford, Carla. 2005. *Smart Moves: Why Learning Is Not All in Your Head*. Salt Lake City, UT: Great River Books.

Harpaz, Beth. 2009. "Preventing high school dropouts can start in 4th grade." *Missourian*, August 12. http://www.columbiamissourian.com/stories/2009/08/12/preventing-hs-dropouts-can-start-4th-grade/.

Heathcote, Dorothy, and Gavin Bolton. 1995. *Drama for Learning*. Portsmouth, NH: Heinemann.

Hetland, Lois, Ellen Winner, Shirley Veenema, and Kimberly M. Sheridan. 2007. *Studio Thinking: The Real Benefits of Visual Arts Education*. New York: Teachers College Press.

Hubbard, Ruth. 1987. "Transferring Images: Not Just Glued on the Page." *Young Children* 42 (2): 60–67.

Intrator, Sam M., and Megan Scribner. 2003. *Teaching with Fire: Poetry That Sustains the Courage to Teach*. San Francisco, CA: Jossey-Bass.

Jacob's Pillow Dance Festival. 2010. "Choreographers Lab 2010: The School at Jacob's Pillow." Program Directors Celeste Miller and Lisa Donovan. YouTube documentation video by Loren R. Robertson. http://www.youtube.com/watch?v=1LZHiHsKG7M.

Janeczko, Paul B. 2011. *Reading Poetry in the Middle Grades: 20 Poems and Activities That Meet the Common Core Standards and Cultivate a Passion for Poetry*. Portsmouth, NH: Heinemann.

Jensen, Eric. 2001. *Arts with the Brain in Mind*. Alexandria, VA: Association for Supervision and Curriculum.

Johnson, Jr., Bob L. 2004. "A Sound Education for All: Multicultural Issues in Music Education." *Educational Policy* 18 (1): 116–141.

Johnson, Thomas H., ed. 1960. *The Complete Poems of Emily Dickinson*. Boston, MA: Little, Brown and Co.

Juster, Norton. 1988. *The Phantom Tollbooth*. New York: Bullseye Books.

Kennedy, Randy. 2006. "Guggenheim Study Suggests Arts Education Benefits Literacy Skills." *The New York Times*, July 27. http://www.nytimes.com/2006/07/27/books/27gugg.html.

King, Nancy, and Jacy Ippolito. 2001. "The Stories Project: Storypartners in the Classroom." *The New Advocate* 14 (1): 69–79.

King, Nancy. 1975. *Giving Form to Feeling*. New York: Drama Book Specialists.

Koch, Kenneth. 1999. *Wishes, Lies, and Dreams: Teaching Children to Write Poetry*. New York: Harper Perennial.

———. 2012. "Rose, Where Did You Get That Red?" Poets. org. Accessed May 31. http://www.poets.org/viewmedia.php/prmMID/17152.

Koki, Stan. 1998. "Storytelling: The Hearts and Soul of Education." PREL Briefing Paper. Honolulu, HI: Pacific Resources for Education and Learning.

Korn, Randi. 2012. "Teaching Literacy Through Art." Solomon R Guggenheim Museum. Accessed June 5. http://www.guggenheim.org/images/lta/pdfs/Executive_Summary_and_Discussion.pdf.

Kozol, Jonathan. 2007. *Letters to a Young Teacher*. New York, Crown Publishers.

Kreiser, Brian, and Rosalina Hairston. 2007. "Dance of the Chromosomes: A Kinetic Leaning Approach to Mitosis and Meiosis." *Bioscene: Journal of College Biology Teaching* 55 (1): 6–10.

Lakoff, George, and Mark Johnson. 2003. *Metaphors We Live By*. Chicago, IL: University of Chicago Press.

Langer, Susanne. 1953. *Feeling and Form: A Theory of Art*. New York: Scribner.

Lansing, Kenneth. 2004. "Why We Need a Definition of Art." Aristos: An Online Review of the Arts. http://www.aristos.org/aris-04/lansing1.htm.

Lesh, Richard A., and Helen Doerr. 2003. *Beyond Constructivism: Models and Modeling Perspectives on Mathematics Problem Solving, Learning, and Teaching*. London: Routledge.

Lippert, Margaret. 2005. "Once Upon a Time, Long Ago: Finding and Adapting Folktales." In *Telling Stories to Children*, edited by B. Lehrman, 37–40. Jonesborough, TN: National Storytelling Press.

Lomax, Alan, ed. 1975. *The Folk Songs of North America.* New York: Doubleday & Company, Inc.

Lovell, Taffy. 2008. "Diamante Poem." Taffy's Writings. Accessed May 31, 2012. http://taffyscandy.blogspot.com/2009/04/diamante-poem.html.

Lowell, Susan. 2000. *Cindy Ellen: A Wild Western Cinderella.* New York: HarperCollins.

Lown, Fredric, and Judith W. Steinbergh. 1996. *Reading and Writing Poetry with Teenagers.* Portland, ME: Walch Publishing.

Lynch, Maureen Ann. 2009. "Making the Relevant Connection: The Middle School Student and Poetry: An Understanding and Appreciation of Poetry to Inspire the Poet Within." Yale National Initiative. Accessed June 11, 2012. http://yale.edu/ynhti/nationalcurriculum/units/2005/1/05.01.03.x.html.

Lyon, George Ella. 2010. "Where I'm From." Accessed March 2, 2010. http://www.georgeellalyon.com/where.html.

MacDonald, Margaret Read. 2006. *Tunjur! Tunjur! Tunjur!: A Palestinian Folktale.* New York: Amazon Children's Publishing.

Mattson, Rachel. 2008. "Theater of the Assess: Drama-based Pedagogies in the History Classroom." *Radical History Review* 2008 (102): 99–110.

Marzano, Robert, Debra Pickering, and Jane Pollock. 2001. *Classroom Instruction that Works: Research-Based Strategies for Increasing Student Achievement.* Alexandria, VA: Association for Supervision and Curriculum Development.

McCabe, Allyssa, and Pamela Rosenthal Rolins. 1994. "Assessment of Preschool Narrative Skills." *American Journal of Speech Language Pathology* 3 (1): 45–56.

McCaslin, Nellie. 2000. *Creative Drama in the Classroom and Beyond*. White Plains, NY: Longman Publishers.

McIntosh, Peggy. 1990. *Interactive Phases of Curricular and Personal Revision with Regard to Race*. Wellesley, MA: Wellesley College Center for Research on Women. 1–18.

McKim, Elizabeth, and Judith W. Steinbergh. 2004. *Beyond Words: Writing Poems with Children*, 3rd ed. Brookline, MA: Talking Stone Press.

Miller, Celeste and J. R. Glover. 2010. "Dancing with Our Textbooks on Our Heads. The Chronicles of Jacob's Pillow Curriculum In Motion® at Monument Mountain Regional High School Told Through Stories, Essays and Strategies for Dance as a Tool for Learning." Unpublished manuscript.

———. 2010. "Unpacking the Kinesthetic Mode for Learning and Teaching: Jacob's Pillow Curriculum in Motion®." Research Findings at Monument Mountain. Unpublished Manuscript.

Minton, Sandra. 2003. "Using Movement to Teach Academics: An Outline for Success." *Journal of Physical Education, Recreation and Dance* 74 (2): 36–40.

Morice, Dave. 1995. *The Adventures of Dr. Alphabet: 104 Unusual Ways to Write Poetry in the Classroom and the Community*. New York: Teachers and Writers Collaborative.

National Governors Association Center for Best Practices and Council of Chief State School Officers. 2011. *Common Core State Standards Initiative: The Standards*. Retrieved June 2011, from Common Core State Standards Initiative. http://www.corestandards.org.

Nemirovsky, Ricardo, and Chris Rasmussen. 2005. "A Case Study of How Kinesthetic Experiences Can Participate in and Transfer to Work With Equations." *Conference of the International Group for the Psychology of Mathematics Education* (9–16). Melbourne, Australia: International Group for the Psychology of Mathematics Education.

Noddings, Nel. 2006. *Critical Lessons: What Our Schools Should Teach.* New York: Cambridge University Press.

Norfolk, Sherry. 2010. "Why Do Teachers Need to Learn About Storytelling?" Unpublished paper.

Northwest Regional Educational Laboratory. 2005. Focus on Effectiveness, "Choreographing Math." Accessed July 17, 2012. http://www.netc.org/focus/examples/choreo.php.

Odegaard, Marianne. 2003. "Dramatic Science. A Critical Review of Drama in Science Education." *Studies in Science Education* 39 (1): 75.101.

O'Neill, Cecily. 1995. *Drama Worlds: A Framework for Process Drama.* Portsmouth, NH: Heinemann.

O'Neill, Cecily, and Alan Lambert. 1991. *Drama Structures: A Practical Handbook for Teachers.* Portsmouth, NH: Heinemann.

Page, Nick. 1995. *Music as a Way of Knowing.* Portland, ME: Stenhouse Publishing.

———. 1995. *Sing and Shine On.* Portsmouth, NH: Heinemann.

Parsons, Michael J., and H. Gene Blocker. 1993. *Aesthetics and Education: Disciplines in Art Education: Contexts of Understanding.* Urbana, IL: University of Illinois Press.

Pascale, Louise. 2002. "Dispelling the Myth of the Non-Singer: Changing the Way Singing Is Perceived, Implemented, and Nurtured in the Classroom." Doctoral dissertation, Lesley University. ProQuest (ATT 3193398).

———. 2005. "Dispelling the Myth of the Non-Singer: Embracing Two Aesthetics for Singing." *Philosophy of Music Education Review* 13 (2): 165–175.

———. 2006. "Finding a Bucket to Carry the Tune: Ways to Shift the Paradigm For Non-Singing Classroom Teachers." *Massachusetts Music News* 40 (1).

Perfect, Kathy A. 1999. "Rhyme and Reason: Poetry from the Heart." *The Reading Teacher* 52 (7): 728–737.

Pink, Daniel H. 2005. *A Whole New Mind*. New York: Riverhead Books.

Plummer, Julia. 2008. "Students' Development of Astronomy Concepts Across Time." *The Astronomy Education Review* 7 (1): 139–148.

Poetry Foundation. "Biography: Kenneth Koch." Poetryfoundation. org. Accessed May 31, 2012. http://www.poetryfoundation. org/bio/kenneth-koch.

Powell, Mary Clare. 1997. "The Arts and the Inner Lives of Teachers." *Phi Delta Kappan* 78 (6): 450–453.

Project Zero. 2006. "Making Learning Visible: Understanding, Documenting, and Supporting Individual and Group Learning." Accessed July 23, 2012. http://www.pz.harvard. edu/mlv/indexfd69.html.

Reeves, Douglas. 2009. "The Value of Culture." *Educational Leadership* 66 (7): 87–89.

Remarque, Erich Maria. 1929. *All Quiet on the Western Front*. Boston, MA: Little Brown and Co.

Rieg, Sue, and Kelli Paquette. 2009. "Using Drama and Movement to Enhance English Language Learners' Literacy Development." *Journal of Instructional Psychology* 36 (2).

Robinson, Ken. "Ken Robinson says schools kill creativity." TED. Filmed February 2006. Accessed June 6, 2012. http://www.ted.com/talks/lang/en/ken_robinson_says_schools_kill_creativity.html.

———. "Ken Robinson: Changing education paradigms." TED. Filmed October 2010. Accessed June 6, 2012. http://www.ted.com/talks/ken_robinson_changing_education_paradigms.html.

Root-Bernstein, Robert, and Michele Root-Bernstein. 1999. *Sparks of Genius: The Thirteen Thinking Tools of the World's Most Creative People.* Boston, MA: Houghton-Mifflin.

Rosler, Brenda. 2008. "Process Drama in One Fifth-grade Social Studies Class." *The Social Studies* 99 (6): 265–272.

Schutzman, Mady, and Jan Cohen-Cruz, eds. 1994. *Playing Boal: Theatre, Therapy, Activism.* New York: Routledge.

Shafak, Elif. 2010. *The Forty Rules of Love: A Novel of Rumi.* New York: Viking Adult.

Sheridan, Susan. 1997. *Drawing/Writing and the New Literacy.* Amherst, MA: Drawing/Writing Publications.

Showalter, Elaine. 2012. "Teaching Poetry." Blackwell Publishing. Accessed May 31. http://www.blackwellpublishing.com/Showalter/SampleChapters.htm.

Silverstein, Lynne B., and Sean Layne. 2010. "Defining Arts Integration." The John F. Kennedy Center for the Performing Arts. Accessed June 11, 2012. https://artsedge. kennedy-center.org/~/media/ArtsEdge/LessonPrintables/ articles/arts-integration/DefiningArtsIntegration.pdf.Sima, Judy. "Storytelling and Science—What a Concept" Michigan Association for Media in Education, Media Spectrum. Accessed June 11, 2012. http://www.judysima.com/pdfs/ Storytelling%20and%20Science.pdf.

Sima, Judy. "Storytelling and Science—What a Concept." Michigan Association for Media in Education, Media Spectrum. Accessed June 11, 2012. http://www.judysima. com/pdfs/Storytelling%20and%20Science.pdf.

Slater, Jana Kay. 2002. "A Poet Came to Our Class." Poetry Evaluation Project, Executive Summary, California Poets in the Schools. Accessed June 11, 2012. http://www.cpits.org/ background/evaluation_study/evaluation.htm.

Stickling, Sara, Melissa Prasun, and Cora Olsen. 2011. "Poetry: What's the Sense in Teaching It?" *Illinois Reading Council Journal* 39 (3): 31–40.

Story Arts. "Why Storytelling?" Storytelling in the Classroom, 2000. Accessed June 1, 2012. http://www.storyarts.org/ classroom/index.html.

Vincent. 2008. "Arctic." Writeshop.com, In Our Write Minds (blog.) Diamante contest winners. Accessed May 31, 2012. http://www.writeshop.com/blog/2008/09/18/diamante-contest-winners/.

Whitin, David J. 1982. "Making Poetry Come Alive." *Language Arts* 60: 456–458.

Wilhelm, Jeffrey, and Brian Edmiston. 1998. *Imagining to Learn: Inquiry, Ethics, and Integration Through Drama.* Portsmouth, NH: Heinemann.

Wilhelm, Jeffrey. 2007. *Language and Literacy: You Gotta BE the Book: Teaching Engaged and Reflective Reading with Adolescents.* New York: Teachers College Press.

Zemelman, Steven, Harvey Daniels, and Arthur Hyde. 1998. *Best Practice: New Standards for Teaching and Learning in America's Schools.* Portsmouth, NH: Heinemann.

Zull, James E. 2002. *The Art of Changing The Brain: Enriching the Practice of Teaching by Exploring the Biology of Learning.* Sterling, VA: Stylus Publishing.